CURRICULUM 2014

Mathematics Assessment Tests

Year 3

Peter Sumner

Acknowledgements:

Author: Peter Sumner
Cover and Page Design: Kathryn Webster

The right of Peter Sumner to be identified as the author of this
publication has been asserted by him in accordance with the
Copyright, Designs and Patents Act 1998.

HeadStart Primary Ltd
Elker Lane
Clitheroe
BB7 9HZ

T. 01200 423405
E. info@headstartprimary.com
www.headstartprimary.com

Published by HeadStart Primary Ltd 2015 © **HeadStart Primary Ltd 2015**

A record for this book is available from the British Library -
ISBN: 978-1-908767-12-7

CONTENTS

HeadStart Primary Mathematics Tests
Teachers' Notes Year 3

Introduction - about the tests

The **HeadStart Primary** Mathematics Tests have been developed to help teachers assess children's progress against the matters, skills and processes (grouped here as 'objectives') contained in the programmes of study for the 2014 maths curriculum.

In Year 3, there are 7 distinct content domains. This is for organisational purposes but the National Curriculum stresses the importance of making necessary mathematical concept connections across the domains.

The domains are:
NUMBER - Number and place value
NUMBER - Addition and subtraction
NUMBER - Multiplication and division
NUMBER - Fractions
MEASUREMENT
GEOMETRY - Properties of shapes
STATISTICS

There are 3 tests for each domain - TEST A, B and C. The content of each test is purposely very similar so that it is possible to assess children's progress over the year, on a like-for-like basis. **It is not intended that all 3 tests are completed for every domain**. Individual schools will choose to organise the delivery of the maths programmes of study in line with their overall curriculum design. The **HeadStart Primary** Tests are designed to fit any curriculum organisation.

It may be, for example, that in Year 3, a school chooses to teach and assess all the 'NUMBER' domains every term, but decides to spread the teaching of MEASUREMENT, GEOMETRY and STATISTICS across the 3 school terms. This could mean that the 4 'NUMBER' domains are tested every term, but the remaining 3 domains are only tested once in each term over the year. This is only one possible model, and all permutations of domain teaching and assessing are available, depending on the requirements of the school.

The tests have been designed to assess a thorough content coverage of each domain. The statutory objectives are assessed, almost without exception. (A small number of objectives are related to a practical activity that cannot be assessed using a paper-based test.)

Much of the non-statutory guidance is also covered and assessed, since this often underpins the conceptual understanding of the statutory objectives. The main purpose of testing should be a formative one, and only a comprehensive coverage of the curriculum can lead to meaningful assessment for learning, performance analysis and future planning.

Timetabling - when to administer the tests

The tests have been designed to provide maximum flexibility regarding when they should be carried out. It is for schools to decide upon the optimum testing frequency in order to facilitate meaningful data analysis, without overloading the curriculum with formal assessments.

Children's progress can be measured against age-related expectations. The system incorporates identification of 6 stages; 2 within 'Expected progress', 2 within 'More than expected progress' and 2 within 'Less than expected progress'.

Progress can be tracked at any time throughout the school year. Although it is possible to track progress after the completion of each test, an overall judgement made every term would present a clear indication of children's performance. The test scores can be recorded and converted for tracking purposes, at an appropriate point, according to the policy of the school. The information gleaned from making a tracking judgement once a term would be wholly appropriate for reporting to parents and as evidence in Ofsted inspections.

Administration - how to manage the tests

Ideally, the class teacher should administer the tests. This gives an overview of the children's performance and a picture of any potential misconceptions as the test is being completed. Observing and making note of the way children approach and tackle the questions can be an extremely useful indicator towards future teaching and learning.

The test papers can be photocopied from the book or printed from the CD-ROM. (It is recommended that page 3 of the MEASUREMENT test is copied from the book; if printed from the disc, printer settings can cause variations in line length which may present a problem for question 7.) The pages are numbered for the benefit of the children completing the test. At the bottom of each page, the year group, domain and test is identified. So, 'Y3: npv - A' is Year 3, NUMBER - Number and place value, TEST A.

A pencil or pen is needed - any other necessary equipment is detailed at the top of the front cover of each test. Since the primary purpose of the tests is formative, no time limits are set for any of the tests.

Support during the tests

When deciding upon the amount of support that is appropriate, it is important to remember that it is maths and not reading that is being tested. If a child needs to have all or some of the test read to them, this support should be made available. However, it is also necessary to avoid giving too much assistance; this could mean that results do not realistically reflect a child's progress in maths.

Teachers have an in-depth knowledge of the children in their care and professional judgement is always the best guide, when considering how much support to provide. It may be that the CD-ROM is used in conjunction with a whiteboard to display and read the pages of the test to a class or group of children. The most successful approach is achieved by developing a whole school agreement/policy on how much support is appropriate for each year group. This ensures effective moderation across the school year groups.

If a child is scoring very low marks consistently, it may be appropriate to administer the corresponding test from a lower year group.

Marking - understanding and using the mark scheme

In Year 3, there are 15 questions in each test. Each question carries a maximum of 2 marks. Ideally, the class teacher should mark the tests. As with the administration of the tests, marking gives a clear picture of necessary next steps on an individual, group and class basis.

Some of the questions have several parts. If the number of parts is even, 1 mark is awarded if half or more of the parts are correct. For example, if a question is comprised of 6 calculations, a child getting 3, 4 or 5 of the calculations correct is awarded 1 mark.

If a question has an odd number of parts, 1 mark is awarded if more than half the parts have a correct answer. For example, a 3-part question would need to have 2 parts correct for the award of 1 mark.

Many questions have only one possible answer but the question still carries 2 marks. Some questions have a definite, correct answer but a child may be awarded 1 mark if appropriate working or method is evident. Since 'appropriate working or method' could involve a number of possible strategies, the final judgement on whether to award one mark has been left to the professional judgement of the teacher.

Tracking - using the tests to track children's progress

Once a test has been marked, a score out of 30 can be awarded. When a tracking judgement is required, test scores should be converted to a percentage (see page 5 Teachers' Notes).

The table below can then be used to identify progress against one of the 6 stages. The table uses percentage scores for conversion, so tracking judgements can be made after any number of tests have been completed.

Year 3

Percentage Score	Stage	
0 - 25	Emerging	Less than expected progress
26 - 50	Developing	
51 - 63	Progressing	Expected progress
64 - 75	Secure	
76 - 88	Mastering	More than expected progress
89 - 100	Exceeding	

0 – 50%	Less than expected
51 – 75%	Expected
76 – 100%	More than expected

Although it is possible to make a tracking judgement after the completion of just one test, this is not recommended. A termly calculation, made after the completion of a number of tests, will provide more reliable information.

The assessment system is intended to be used by teachers as a tool to support their professional judgement.

Using the percentage scoring model to make a tracking judgement

An example

A Year 3 teacher has decided to make a tracking judgement for the children in the class at the end of the autumn term. The children have been taught the content for the following domains and the tests (TEST A versions) have been completed:

NUMBER - Number and place value
NUMBER - Addition and subtraction
NUMBER - Multiplication and division
MEASUREMENT

Step 1 Add together the test scores for each child.

Step 2 Find the overall percentage score for each child.

Step 3 Identify the stage achieved from the percentage score.

This means that a Year 3 child scoring as follows:

NUMBER - Number and place value   (19 out of 30)

NUMBER - Addition and subtraction   (20 out of 30)

NUMBER - Multiplication and division   (17 out of 30)

MEASUREMENT   (20 out of 30)

has a total score of **76 out of 120**

Percentage score $= (\dfrac{76}{120} \times 100) =$ **63%**

Therefore, a child scoring 63% is working at the 'Expected' level in the 'Progressing' stage. (It is worth noting that the child is close to achieving the 'Secure' stage.)

NB: This data should always be used in conjunction with ongoing teacher assessment.

Analysis and assessment for learning - using the objectives grids and pupil objective record sheets to identify strengths and weaknesses

Every test question is underpinned by a statutory objective or an objective from the non-statutory notes and guidance. There is an objectives grid for each test, on which children's performance can be recorded. The grids can be enlarged to A3 to make recording easier and clearer.

The objectives have been labelled to match the bullet points in the Year 3 Programmes of Study as follows:

NUMBER - Number and place value	(npv	1 – 6)
NUMBER - Addition and subtraction	(as	1 – 4)
NUMBER - Multiplication and division	(md	1 – 3)
NUMBER - Fractions	(f	1 – 7)
MEASUREMENT	(m	1 – 7)
GEOMETRY - Properties of shapes	(g	1 – 4)
STATISTICS	(s	1 – 2)

The pupil objective record sheet can be used to measure individual performance against each national curriculum objective.

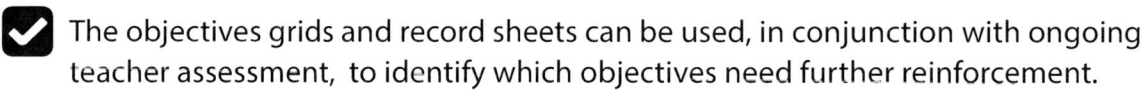 The objectives grids and record sheets can be used, in conjunction with ongoing teacher assessment, to identify which objectives need further reinforcement.

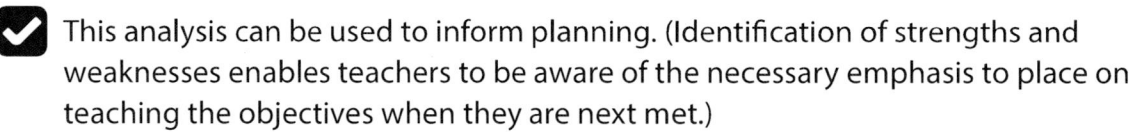 This analysis can be used to inform planning. (Identification of strengths and weaknesses enables teachers to be aware of the necessary emphasis to place on teaching the objectives when they are next met.)

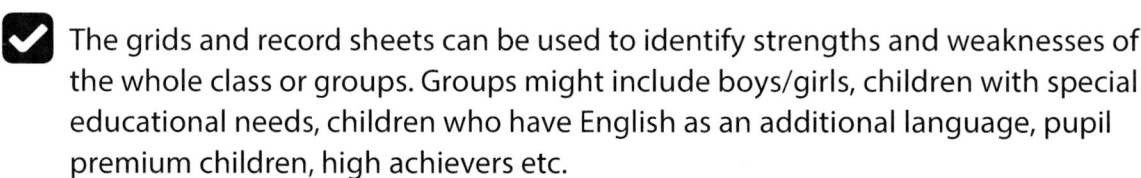 The grids and record sheets can be used to identify strengths and weaknesses of the whole class or groups. Groups might include boys/girls, children with special educational needs, children who have English as an additional language, pupil premium children, high achievers etc.

Test analysis software is also available from **HeadStart Primary**. Tests can be marked directly into the software; detailed performance analysis is then automatically generated for individuals, groups and classes.

Please visit **www.headstartprimary.com** for more information.

Mathematics Assessment: NUMBER - Number and place value

Name.............................. Class..................... Date.....................

1 Complete the number patterns below.

a   0   4   [   ]   [12]   [16]   [   ]

b   0   50   [   ]   [150]   [200]   [   ]

c   0   8   [   ]   [24]   [32]   [   ]

2 marks

2 Aftab is counting forward in tens. He starts at **87**, then counts on **3** more tens.

What number does he count up to? [   ]

2 marks

3 Nicola is counting backwards in hundreds. She starts at **974**, then counts back **3** more hundreds.

What number does she count back to? [   ]

2 marks

4 Complete the following. Work out the answers in your head.

a   28 + 10   = [   ]   **d**   649 + 100 = [   ]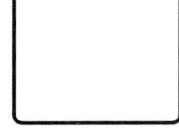

b   46 - 10   = [   ]   **e**   758 - 100   = [   ]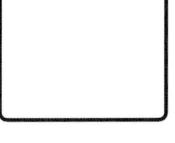

c   684 + 10 = [   ]   **f**   125 - 100   = [   ]

2 marks

Page Total ◯

5 Complete the following.

a) What is the value of the digit **4** in the number **489**? [ ]

b) What is the value of the digit **3** in the number **263**? [ ]

c) What is the value of the digit **7** in the number **675**? [ ]

2 marks

6 Put the following numbers in order of size, starting with the smallest.

	smallest		largest

a) 96   32   23   [ ] [ ] [ ]

b) 264   196   482   [ ] [ ] [ ]

c) 819   918   189   [ ] [ ] [ ]

2 marks

7 Partition **357** in different ways by filling in the boxes below.

a) 357 = [300] + [50] + [ ]

b) 357 = [300] + [ ] + [17]

c) 357 = [200] + [ ] + [7]

2 marks

Page Total ◯

8 Match the words to the correct figures. One has been done for you.

a) twelve　　　　　　　　　　　　　56

b) three　　　　　　　　　　　　　12

c) fifty six　　　　　　　　　　　　3

d) sixty five　　　　　　　　　　　522

e) five hundred and twenty two　　24

f) twenty four　　　　　　　　　　65

9 Write the following numbers in words. For example, **236** would be 'two hundred and thirty six'.

a) 64　...

b) 197　..

c) 864　..

d) 608　..

Page Total

10 Fill in the missing numbers to complete the number statements below.

a   16   +   ☐   =   23

b   ☐6   +   7   =   33

c   3☐   +   7   =   43

2 marks

11 Joe puts **200 grams** of flour into a bowl. He then adds another **6** tablespoons of flour, each containing **10 grams**.

How many grams of flour are in the bowl now?

Show your working out in this this box.

☐ grams

2 marks

Y3: npv-A

Page Total ◯

12 Look at the *pattern* in the calculations below.

a What is the next answer in the pattern?

$$172 \quad + \quad 200 \quad = \quad 372$$

$$172 \quad + \quad 400 \quad = \quad 572$$

$$172 \quad + \quad 600 \quad = \quad 772$$

$$172 \quad + \quad 800 \quad = \quad \boxed{}$$

b Explain how the pattern helps you to answer the question. Use the box below.

2 marks

13 Add together the value of the digit **3** in the number **396** to the value of the digit **8** in the number **487**.

Show your working out in this this box.

2 marks

Page Total

14 Mr Jones saved up **468** pound coins in a big bottle. He emptied the bottle and gave **£200** to Mrs Jones, **£10** to Jonathan and **£10** to Jessica.

How much did Mr Jones have left?

Show your working out in this this box.

£

2 marks

15 Sienna has a secret number. It has **2** digits and it is a multiple of **8**. The digits add up to **10**.

What is Sienna's number?

2 marks

End of Test

Page Total

TEST TOTAL

30

PERCENTAGE SCORE

%

Mathematics Assessment: NUMBER - Addition and subtraction

Name... Class......................... Date........................

1 Complete the following. Use a *mental* method that you know.

a 53 + 6 = ☐   **d** 59 - 7 = ☐

b 8 + 45 = ☐   **e** 80 - 9 = ☐

c 9 + 88 = ☐   **f** 94 - 8 = ☐

2 marks

2 Complete the following. Use a *mental* method that you know.

a 23 + 34 = ☐   **c** 38 + 56 = ☐

b 96 - 45 = ☐   **d** 180 - 14 = ☐

2 marks

3 Compete the following. Use a *mental* method that you know.

a 276 + 3 = ☐   **d** 896 - 4 = ☐

b 849 + 1 = ☐   **e** 690 - 1 = ☐

c 638 + 9 = ☐   **f** 363 - 4 = ☐

2 marks

4 Compete the following. Use a *mental* method that you know.

a 364 + 20 = ☐   **d** 693 - 20 = ☐

b 832 + 40 = ☐   **e** 248 - 30 = ☐

c 642 + 50 = ☐   **f** 974 - 70 = ☐

2 marks

---

5 Complete the following. Use a *mental* method that you know.

a 498 + 100 = ☐   **d** 843 - 100 = ☐

b 632 + 300 = ☐   **e** 586 - 200 = ☐

c 756 + 300 = ☐   **f** 863 - 700 = ☐

2 marks

---

6 Use a *written* method of column addition to solve the following.

a 252 + 39 = ☐   **b** 346 + 468 = ☐

Set out your calculations in this box.

2 marks

Page Total ◯

7 Use a **written** method of column subtraction to solve the following.

a 94 - 38 = ☐   **b** 632 - 358 = ☐

Set out your calculations in this box.

2 marks

8 Use a **written** method of column addition to solve the following.

a 36 + 472 + 6 = ☐   **b** 17 + 83 + 598 = ☐

Set out your calculations in this box.

2 marks

Page Total ◯

9 Ameer wants to estimate the answer to **22 + 87**.

Circle the sum which is the best estimation.

$$20 + 80 \qquad\qquad 30 + 90 \qquad\qquad 20 + 90$$

2 marks

---

10 Isobel thought that **347 + 485 = 832**.

Fill in the boxes below to show a different number statement that she could use to check her calculation.

$$\boxed{} \quad - \quad 485 \quad = \quad \boxed{}$$

2 marks

---

11 Complete the number statements below by putting one digit in each box. An example is done for you.

example $\boxed{1}\ \boxed{9} - \boxed{7} = 12$

a $\boxed{}\boxed{} - \boxed{} = 13$

b $\boxed{}\boxed{} - \boxed{} = 15$

c $\boxed{}\boxed{} - \boxed{} = 19$

2 marks

Y3: as-A

Page Total

12 **27 + 27 = 54**. Explain how this fact helps you know that **27 + 28 = 55**.

Use this box to explain.

13 Add the value of the digit **4** in the number **249** to the value of the digit **6** in the number **638**. Use the boxes below.

$$\boxed{} + \boxed{} = \boxed{}$$

14 Jake is **132 cm** tall. He puts on his hat which makes him **4 cm** taller. Marshall is **120 cm** tall.

How much taller is Jake (with his hat on) than Marshall?

Show your working out in this box.

cm

Y3: as-A

Page Total

15 Ruby has a one litre carton of milk. She pours two glasses of milk from the carton. One glass has **190 ml** of milk and the other has **210 ml** of milk.

How much milk is left *in the carton?*

Show your working out in this box.

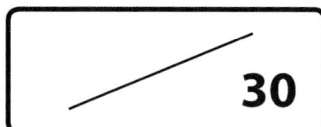

ml

2 marks

End of Test

TEST TOTAL

30

PERCENTAGE SCORE

%

Y3: as-A

Mathematics Assessment: NUMBER - Multiplication and division

Name .... Class .... Date ....

1 Complete the following as quickly as you can.

a) 2×3 = ☐   d) $24 \div 3$ = ☐

b) 12×3 = ☐   e) $3 \div 3$ = ☐

c) 6×3 = ☐   f) $21 \div 3$ = ☐

2 marks

2 Complete the following as quickly as you can.

a) 5×4 = ☐   d) $48 \div 4$ = ☐

b) 9×4 = ☐   e) $8 \div 4$ = ☐

c) 7×4 = ☐   f) $32 \div 4$ = ☐

2 marks

3 Complete the following as quickly as you can.

a) 7×8 = ☐   d) $64 \div 8$ = ☐

b) 12×8 = ☐   e) $72 \div 8$ = ☐

c) 5×8 = ☐   f) $88 \div 8$ = ☐

2 marks

Y3: md-A

Page Total ◯

4 Complete the pattern below.

a

$$6 \times 2 = 12$$

$$6 \times 4 = 24$$

$$6 \times 8 = \boxed{}$$

b Imagine that the **8** times tables has been banned.

How can you work out **6 x 8** if you know that **6 x 4 = 24**?

Use this box to explain.

5 Complete the following. Use a *mental* method that you know.

a 23 x 3 = $\boxed{}$ **d** 69 ÷ 3 = $\boxed{}$

b 32 x 4 = $\boxed{}$ **e** 84 ÷ 4 = $\boxed{}$

c 51 x 8 = $\boxed{}$ **f** 96 ÷ 8 = $\boxed{}$

Y3: md-A

Page Total

6 Fill in the missing numbers.

a   3   x   4   x   8   =   □

b   8   x   □   x   4   =   96

2 marks

---

7 Fill in the missing number.

4   x   5   x   12   =   240

so   □   x   12   =   240

2 marks

---

8 *Circle* the number statement which could help you solve **80 ÷ 20**.

$2 \times 8 = 16$ $8 \div 2 = 4$ $4 \div 8 = 2$

2 marks

---

9 Use a *written* method of multiplication to solve the following.

a   26 x 3   =   □   **b**   43 x 8   =   □

Set out your calculations in this box.

2 marks

Page Total

10 Use a **written** method of division to solve the following.

a 84 ÷ 4 = ⬚   **b** 968 ÷ 8 = ⬚

Set out your calculations in this box.

---

11 A cricket bat measures **68 cm**.

Use a **written** method of **multiplication** to find the length of **4** cricket bats placed end to end.

Show your working out in this box.

cm

12 A tin of biscuits has **96** biscuits in **4** layers.

Use a **written** method of **division** to find how many biscuits are in each layer.

Show your working out in this box.

biscuits

2 marks

---

13 Leroy made a model of a tree house that was **76 cm** high. Leroy's dad built the real tree house four times as high as the model.

How high was the real tree house?

Show your working out in this box.

cm

2 marks

Page Total

14 You can stick **4** different noses and **3** different mouths onto Mr Potato Head.

How many different Mr Potato Heads can you make altogether?

Show your working out in this box.

Mr Potato Heads

2 marks

---

15 The theme park ride, the Big Gripper, takes **8** people on one ride.

How many rides are needed so that **896** people can have a turn?

Show your working out in this box.

rides

2 marks

End of Test

Page Total

TEST TOTAL

PERCENTAGE SCORE

/ 30

%

Y3: md-A

Mathematics Assessment: NUMBER - Fractions

Name .... Class .... Date ....

1 Complete the patterns by writing the missing fractions in the boxes.

a

$\dfrac{3}{10}$	$\dfrac{}{}$	$\dfrac{5}{10}$	$\dfrac{6}{10}$	$\dfrac{7}{10}$

b

$\dfrac{9}{10}$	$\dfrac{8}{10}$	$\dfrac{7}{10}$	$\dfrac{}{}$	$\dfrac{5}{10}$

2 marks

---

2 Look at the shape below.

a How many tenths are shaded?

$\boxed{ \text{tenths}}$

b Now complete the shading on the shape so that **six tenths** of the shape are shaded.

2 marks

Y3: f-A

1

Page Total

3 Match the fractions to the decimals. One has been done for you.

a   0.7

b   0.1

c   0.3

d   0.8

$\dfrac{8}{10}$

$\dfrac{3}{10}$

$\dfrac{7}{10}$

$\dfrac{1}{10}$

4 Complete the following.

a $6 \div 10 = $ ▢

b $7 \div 10 = $ ▢

c $9 \div 10 = $ ▢

Remember,
8 divided by
10 is 0.8

Y3: f-A

Page Total

5 What fraction of the buttons is in the ring?

Circle your answer.

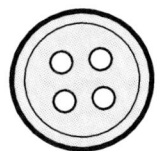 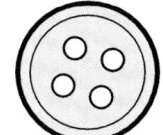

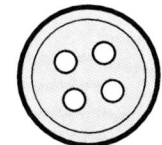

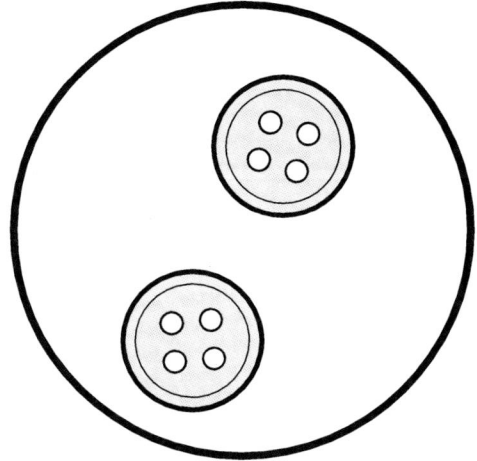

$$\frac{3}{5}$$ $$\frac{2}{5}$$

$$\frac{5}{6}$$ $$\frac{1}{5}$$

2 marks

---

6 Draw an arrow (↓) pointing to **5½** on the number line.

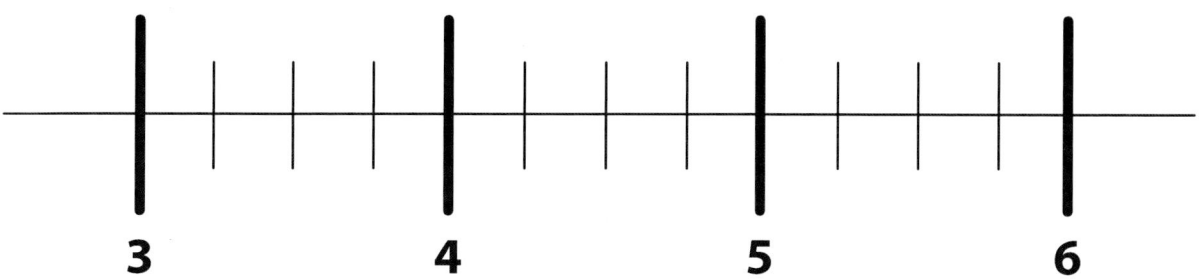

3   4   5   6

2 marks

Y3: f-A

Page Total

7 Look at Declan's pizza.

How much has he eaten? Write your answer as a *fraction*.

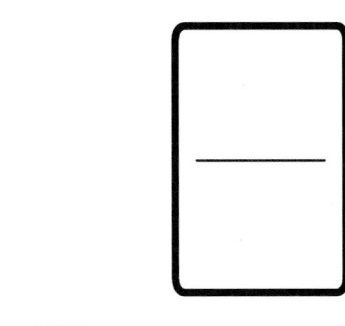

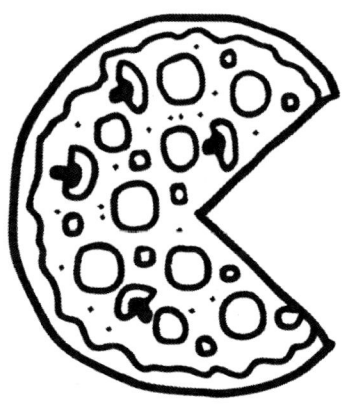

2 marks

---

8 Which is more? Tick (✔) the box.

| $\dfrac{1}{2}$ of 16 litres | **or** | $\dfrac{1}{4}$ of 28 litres |

2 marks

---

9 Complete the following.

a $\dfrac{1}{5}$ of 25 = ☐

b $\dfrac{1}{4}$ of 28 = ☐

2 marks

Y3: f-A

Page Total

10 Match the equal fractions. One has been done for you.

a

$$\frac{1}{2}$$

$$\frac{2}{10}$$

b

$$\frac{1}{3}$$

$$\frac{2}{8}$$

c

$$\frac{1}{4}$$

$$\frac{2}{4}$$

d

$$\frac{1}{5}$$

$$\frac{2}{6}$$

2 marks

---

11 Shade some of shape **B** to match shape **A**.

A

B

2 marks

Page Total

12 Complete the following.

(a) $\dfrac{1}{5} + \dfrac{3}{5} = \boxed{\dfrac{}{}}$

(b) $\dfrac{2}{7} + \dfrac{3}{7} = \boxed{\dfrac{}{}}$

2 marks

13 Complete the following.

(a) $\dfrac{7}{8} - \dfrac{4}{8} = \boxed{\dfrac{}{}}$

(b) $\dfrac{5}{6} - \dfrac{2}{6} = \boxed{\dfrac{}{}}$

2 marks

14 Put these fractions in order of size, starting with the smallest.

(a) $\dfrac{5}{6}$ $\dfrac{2}{6}$ $\dfrac{4}{6}$ $\dfrac{3}{6}$

$\boxed{\dfrac{}{}}$ $\boxed{\dfrac{}{}}$ $\boxed{\dfrac{}{}}$ $\boxed{\dfrac{}{}}$

smallest   **largest**

(b) $\dfrac{1}{4}$ $\dfrac{1}{2}$ $\dfrac{1}{12}$ $\dfrac{1}{9}$

$\boxed{\dfrac{}{}}$ $\boxed{\dfrac{}{}}$ $\boxed{\dfrac{}{}}$ $\boxed{\dfrac{}{}}$

smallest   **largest**

2 marks

Y3: f-A

Page Total

15 On Tuesday, Rukaya ate **two fifths** of her birthday cake.

On Wednesday, she ate another $\frac{1}{5}$ of her cake.

How much did she eat on Tuesday and Wednesday altogether?

Use this box if you need to do any working out.

She ate ⬜ of her cake

on Tuesday and Wednesday altogether.

End of Test

Page Total ⬤

TEST TOTAL

/ 30

PERCENTAGE SCORE

%

Y3: f-A

Mathematics Assessment: MEASUREMENT

Name .... Class .... Date ....

1 What length is the arrow showing?

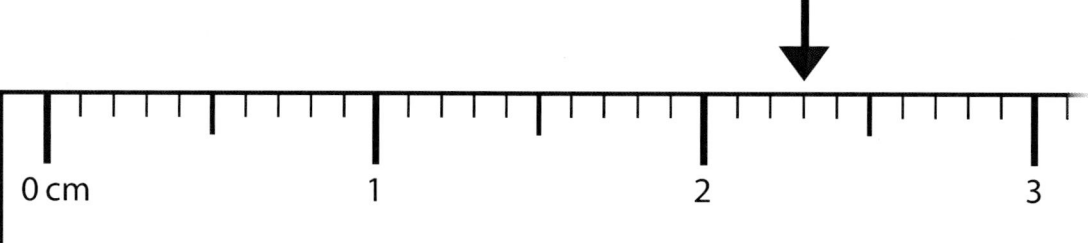

_____cm _____mm

2 marks

2 What measurement is shown on the scales?

_____ kg

2 marks

3 Joy is **1 m 34 cm** tall and Nik is **143 cm** tall. Who is taller?

Use this box if you need to do any working out.

_____ is taller

2 marks

Y3: m-A

Page Total

4 How much water is in the measuring jug?

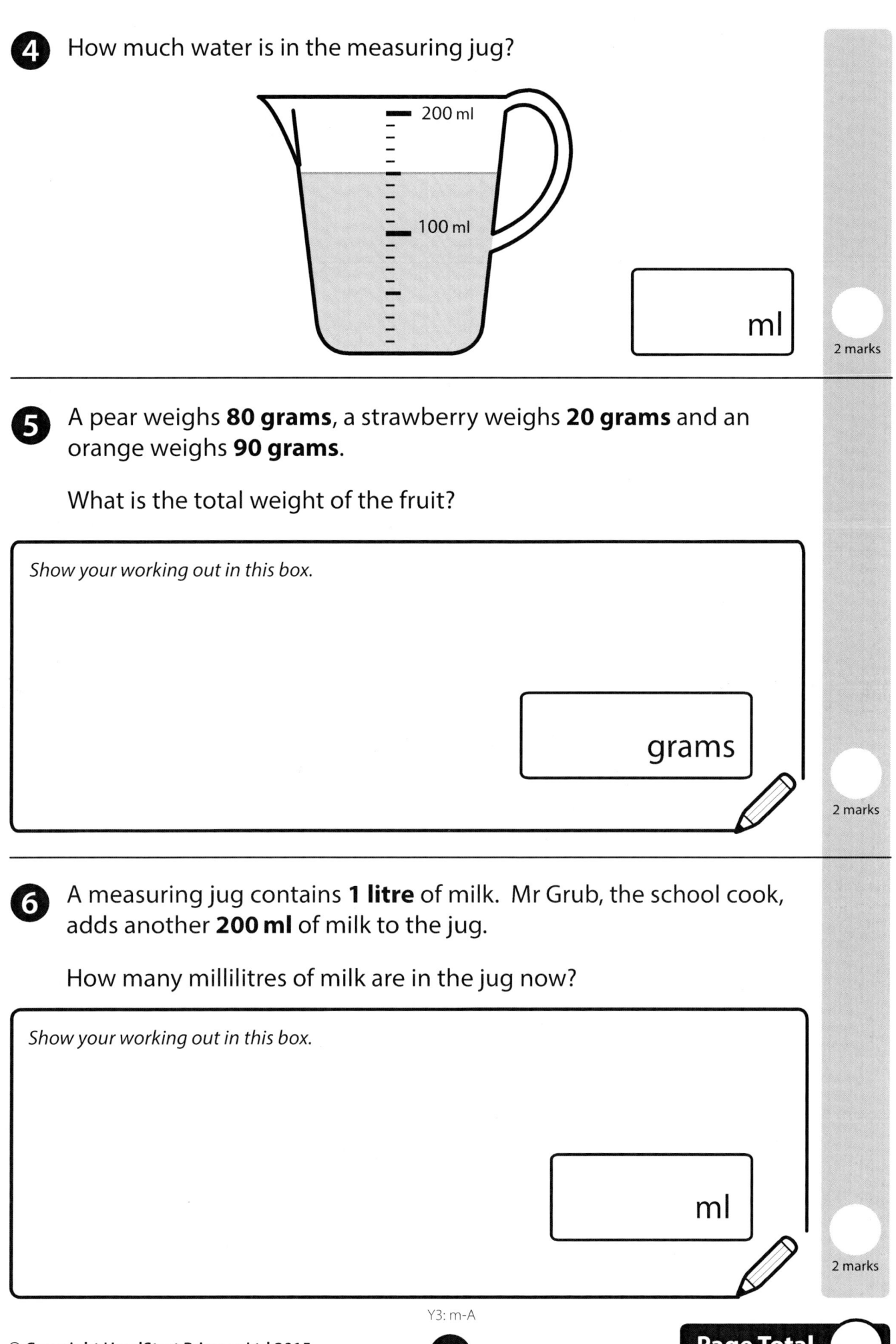

[ ] ml

2 marks

---

5 A pear weighs **80 grams**, a strawberry weighs **20 grams** and an orange weighs **90 grams**.

What is the total weight of the fruit?

Show your working out in this box.

[ ] grams

2 marks

---

6 A measuring jug contains **1 litre** of milk. Mr Grub, the school cook, adds another **200 ml** of milk to the jug.

How many millilitres of milk are in the jug now?

Show your working out in this box.

[ ] ml

2 marks

Y3: m-A

Page Total ◯

7 Use your ruler to measure the **perimeter** of the rectangle below.

The perimeter measures [ ] cm

2 marks

8 In a fish and chip shop, fish costs **£2.75** and chips cost **£1.00**.

If Caitlyn buys fish and chips, how much change will she get from **£5.00**?

Show your working out in this box.

£ [ ]

2 marks

9 Tom has **five £1** coins, **three 20p** coins and **two 10p** coins.

How much does he have altogether?

Show your working out in this box.

£ [ ]

2 marks

Y3: m-A

Page Total

10 What time is it?

Write your answers in the boxes below the clocks.

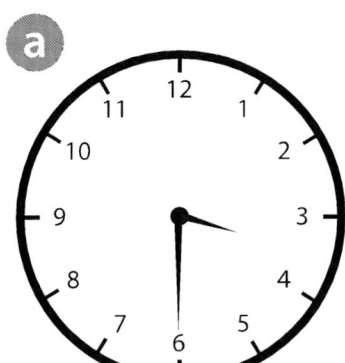
a

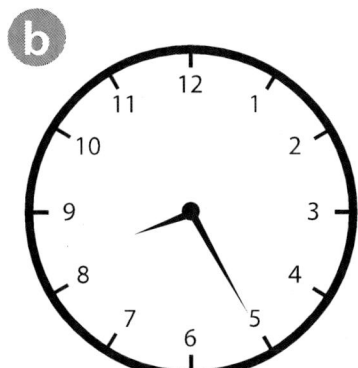
b

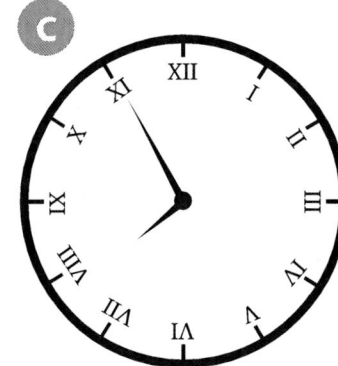
c

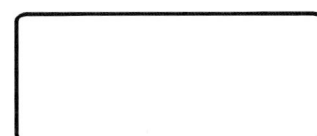

2 marks

---

11 Draw the times shown on the clocks below.

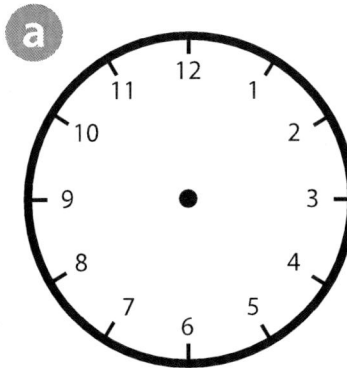
a

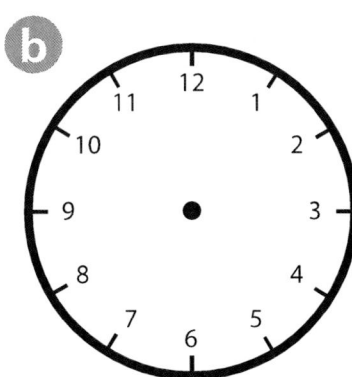
b

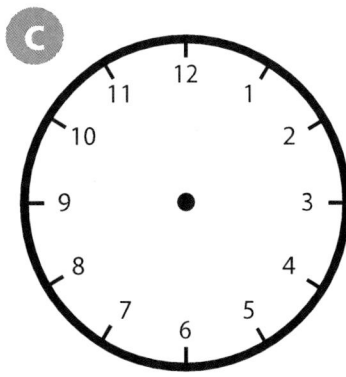
c

| four o'clock | 11:30 am | 18:00 |

2 marks

Y3: m-A

Page Total

12 Khadeeja started skipping at the time shown on clock **A.**

She stopped at the time shown on clock **B.**

Estimate how many minutes she skipped for.

A

B

┌─────────────────┐
│   │
│   minutes │
│   │
└─────────────────┘

2 marks

---

13 Write **TRUE (T)** or **FALSE (F)** after these statements.

a When it's afternoon, it's **am**.

b When it's afternoon, it's **pm**.

c Noon and midnight are 10 hours apart.

2 marks

Y3: m-A

Page Total

14 Find the matching pairs below. Join them with a line. One has been done for you.

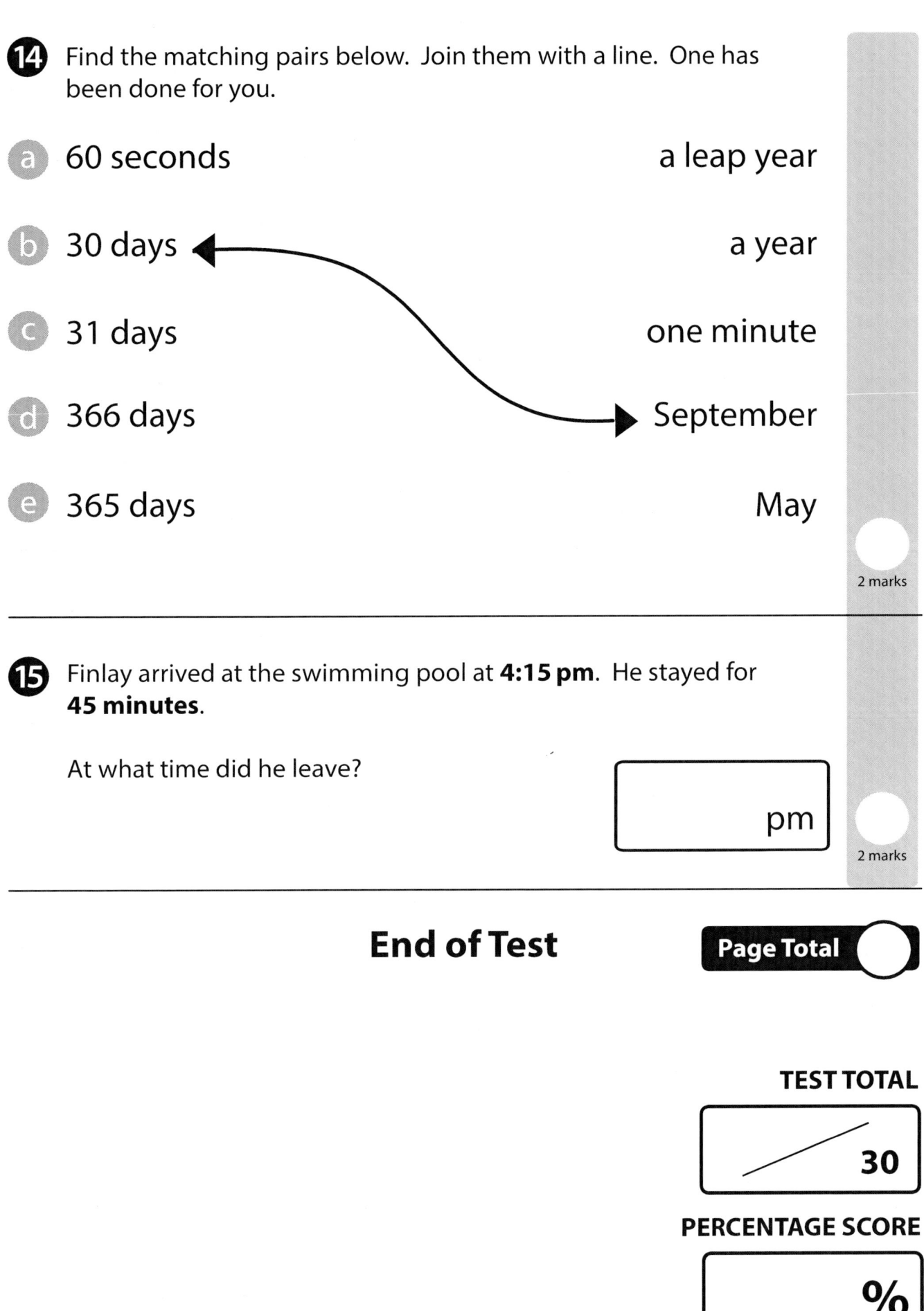

a 60 seconds   a leap year

b 30 days   a year

c 31 days   one minute

d 366 days   September

e 365 days   May

2 marks

---

15 Finlay arrived at the swimming pool at **4:15 pm**. He stayed for **45 minutes**.

At what time did he leave?

⬜ pm

2 marks

End of Test

Page Total ◯

Y3: m-A

TEST TOTAL

⬜ 30

PERCENTAGE SCORE

⬜ %

Mathematics Assessment: GEOMETRY - Properties of shapes

Name.. Class......................... Date........................

1   Use your ruler to draw a rectangle in the space below.

2 marks

2   Hamza drew a line **9.5 cm** long as one side of his rectangle. He then decided to round the length of the line up to the next whole number.

How long was Hamza's line after rounding?

[cm]

2 marks

3   Match the 3D shapes to their names. One has been done for you.

a   pyramid   b   cube   c   cylinder   d   cuboid

2 marks

4 Match the 2D or 3D shapes to their description. One has been done for you.

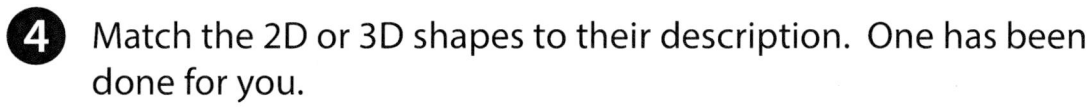

a hexagon

b sphere

c triangle

d prism

e square

a 3D shape with **2** triangular faces and **3** rectangular faces

a 2D shape with **3** sides and **3** angles

a 2D shape with **6** sides, **6** angles and **6** lines of symmetry

a 2D shape with **4** equal sides and **4** equal angles

a 3D shape that is round like a football

2 marks

Y3: g-A

2

Page Total

5 Choose **one** word from the brackets to complete the sentence below.

Angles are a _____ of shapes.

(section, property, kind)

2 marks

---

6 Choose **one** word from the brackets to complete the sentence below.

Angles show an amount of _____ .

(turn, weight, length)

2 marks

---

7 Lucas is facing east. He then turns to face west.

How many **right angles** has he turned through?

right angles

2 marks

Y3: g-A

Page Total

8 Look at the shape below. Put a tick (✓) next to the right angle.

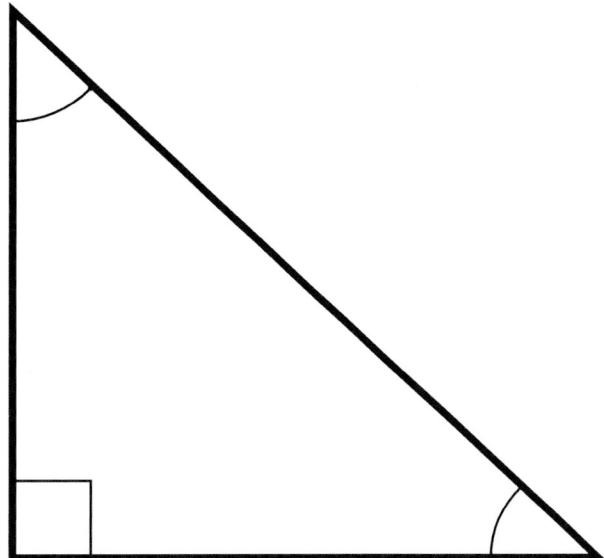

9 Write **TRUE (T)** or **FALSE (F)** after these statements.

a Four right angles make a half-turn.

b One right angle makes a quarter-turn.

c Three right angles make three-quarters of a turn.

d Two right angles make a complete turn.

Y3: g-A

Page Total

10 Are the angles below greater than or less than a right angle?

Write '**greater**' or '**less**' in the boxes.

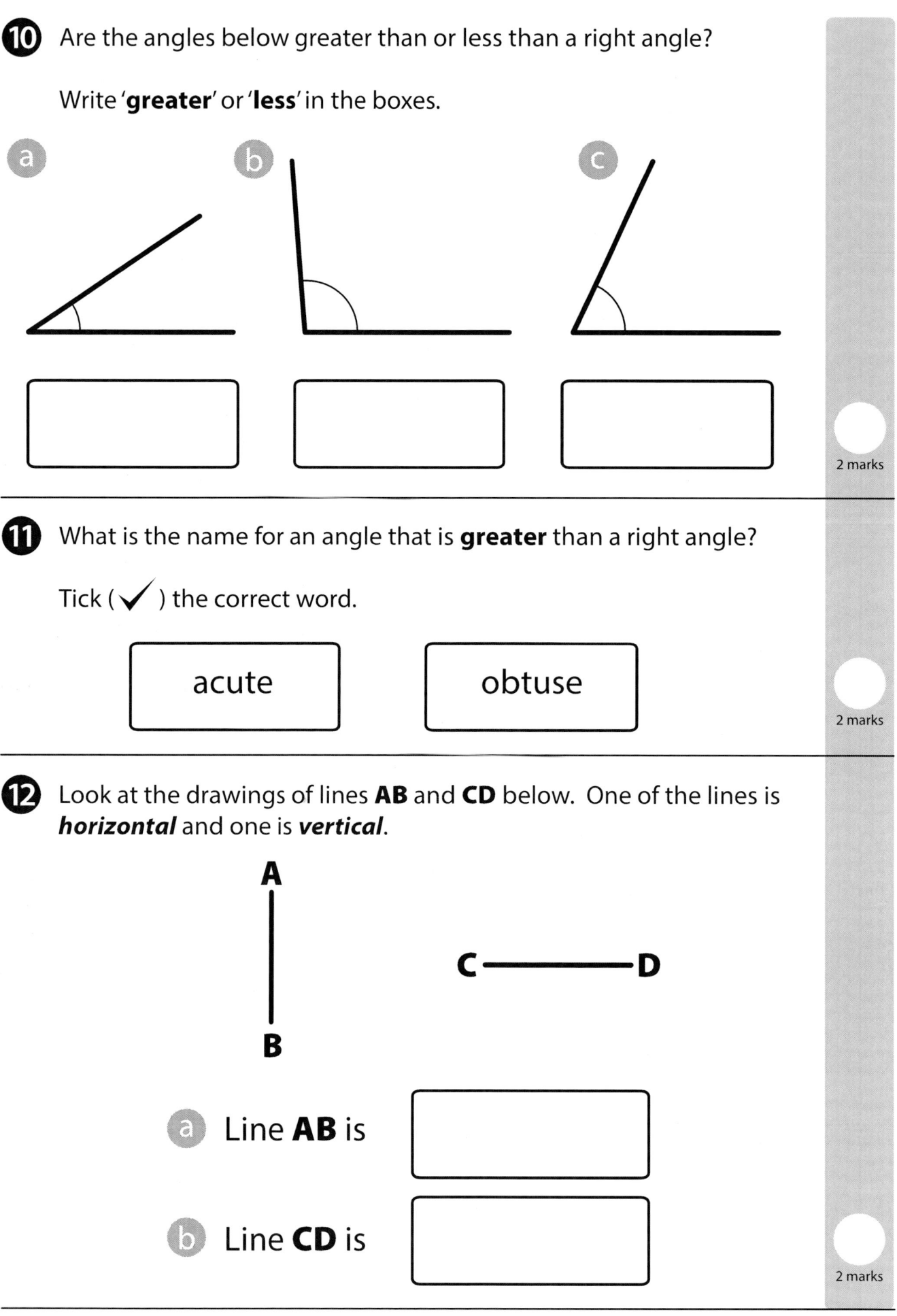

a

b

c

2 marks

---

11 What is the name for an angle that is **greater** than a right angle?

Tick (✓) the correct word.

acute		obtuse

2 marks

---

12 Look at the drawings of lines **AB** and **CD** below. One of the lines is *horizontal* and one is *vertical*.

A
|
B

C——————D

a Line **AB** is

b Line **CD** is

2 marks

Y3: g-A

Page Total

13 In the space below, use your ruler to draw a line that is *perpendicular* to line **AB**.

A ——————————————————————————— B

2 marks

14 In the space below, use your ruler to draw a line that is *parallel* to line **AB**.

A ——————————————————————————— B

2 marks

Y3: g-A

Page Total

15 Write **TRUE (T)** or **FALSE (F)** after these statements.

a Perpendicular lines are always at right angles to each other.

b Two parallel lines will never meet.

c A horizontal line goes straight up and down.

d A vertical line goes from left to right.

2 marks

End of Test

Page Total

TEST TOTAL

/ 30

PERCENTAGE SCORE

%

Y3: g-A

Mathematics Assessment: STATISTICS

Name... Class....................... Date.......................

Look at the bar chart below.

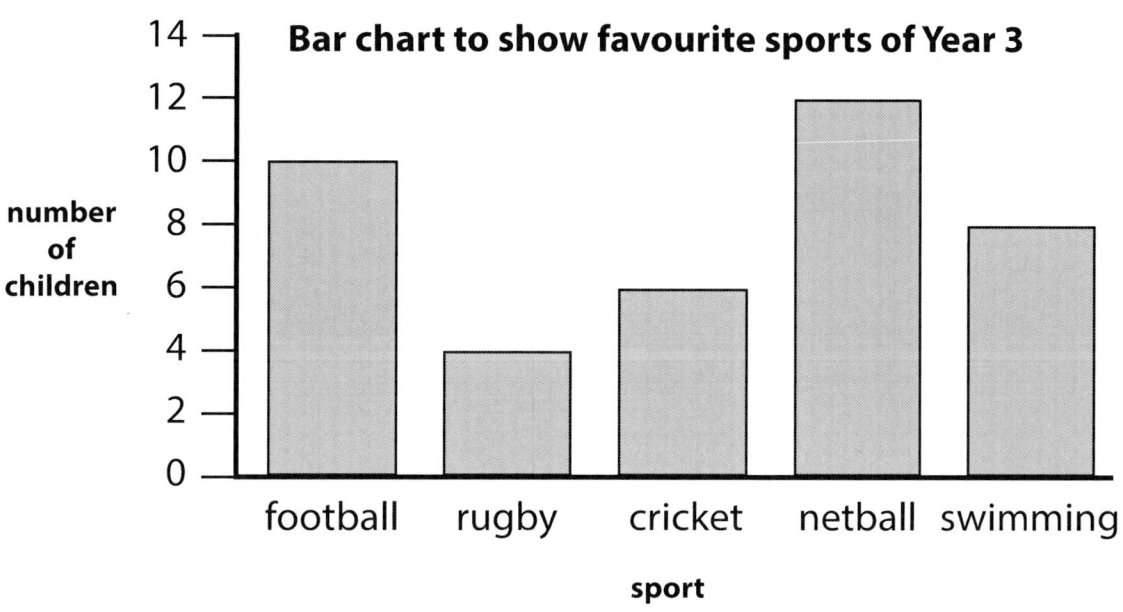

Bar chart to show favourite sports of Year 3

number of children

football   rugby   cricket   netball   swimming

sport

Now answer these questions.

1 What is the most popular sport in Year 3?

2 marks

2 How many more people like netball than rugby?

people

2 marks

3 If **3** people changed their mind and said they liked cricket and not football, how many more people would like cricket than football?

people

2 marks

Page Total

Look at the tally chart below.

Animals on the farm

Animal		Tally
horses		|||| ||
cows		|||
sheep		||||
pigs		|||| ||||

Now answer these questions.

4 How many cows are on the farm?

[ ] COWS

5 How many more horses are there than cows?

[ ]

6 Florence says, "There are more pigs than there are cows and sheep put together".

Is that true? (Yes or No)

[ ]

Use this box to explain how you know.

2 marks

Y3: s-A

© Copyright HeadStart Primary Ltd 2015

2

Page Total ◯

Look at the pictogram below.

Pictogram to show colour of bikes sold in a week

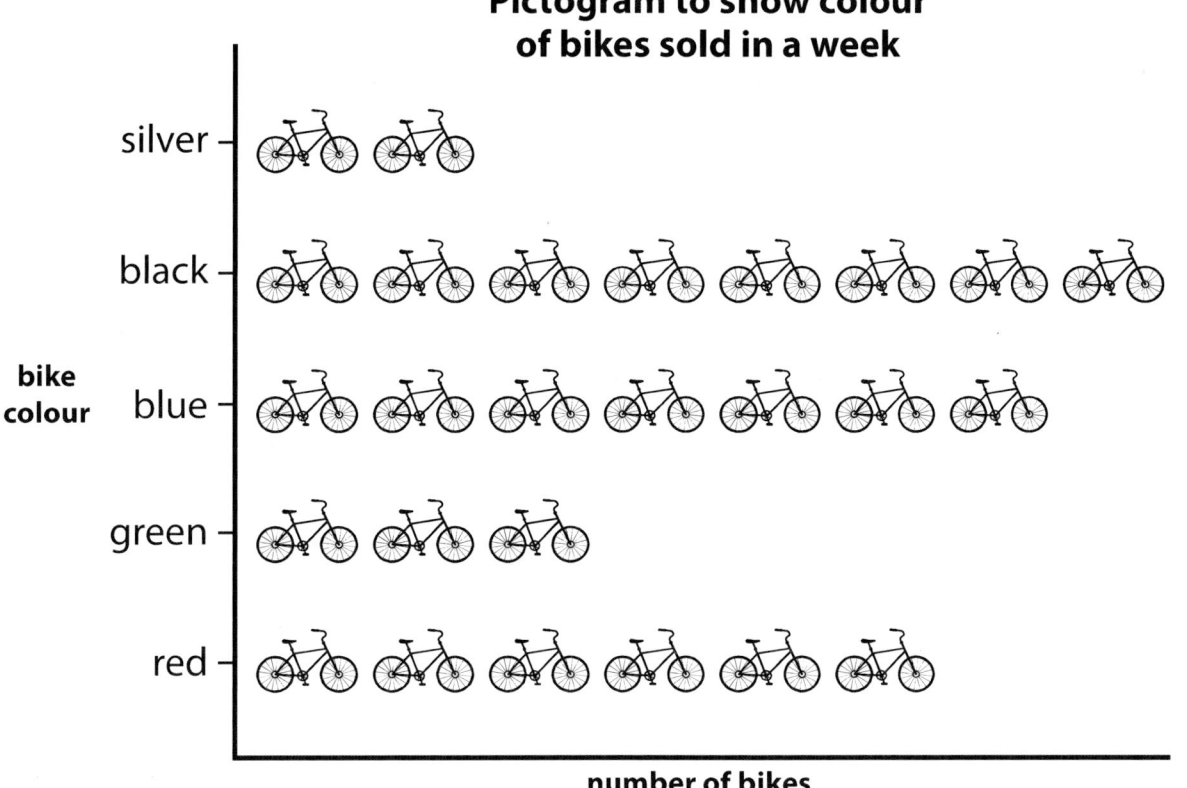

bike colour

silver

black

blue

green

red

number of bikes

Now answer these questions.

7 How many silver and blue bikes are sold altogether?

8 How many more blue bikes are sold than green bikes?

9 During the next week, black, blue and red bikes sold the same amount as shown on the pictogram. Silver sold **3** more and green sold **2** more.

Draw more bikes on the pictogram to show this information.

Page Total

Look at the frequency table below.

Day	Number of cars in the car park
Monday	11
Tuesday	13
Wednesday	17
Thursday	6
Friday	12

Now answer these questions.

10 How many cars were in the car park on Friday?

cars

2 marks

11 How many more cars were there on Wednesday than on Thursday?

cars

2 marks

12 Using the information in the table, write a question that you could ask about the cars in the car park.

Write your question in this box.

2 marks

Y3: s-A

Page Total

13 Look at the bar chart below.

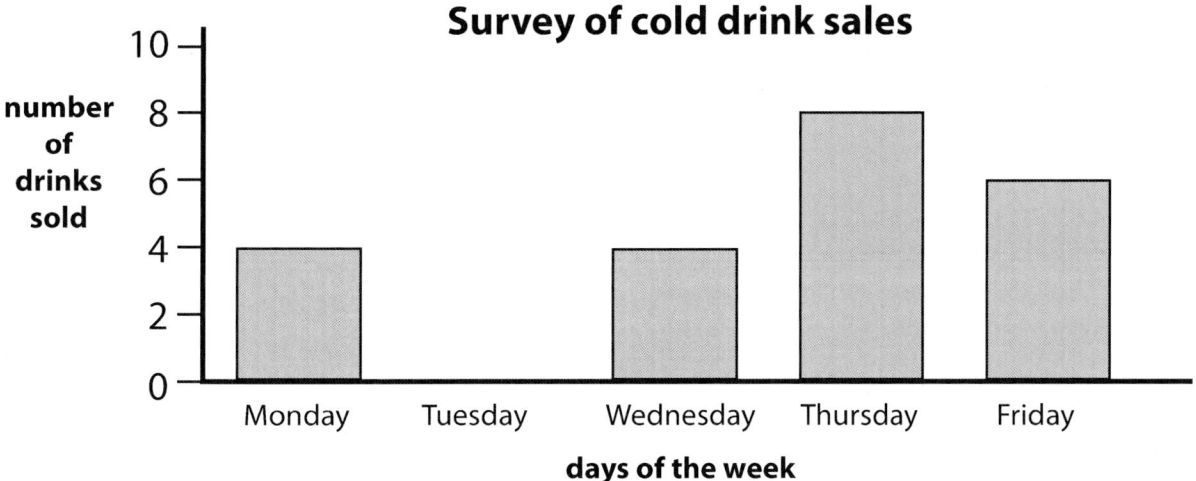

Survey of cold drink sales

number of drinks sold

10
8
6
4
2
0

Monday Tuesday Wednesday Thursday Friday

days of the week

a Firstly, draw in a bar to show that **8** cold drinks were sold on Tuesday.

b Now work out how many cold drinks were sold all week.

Use this box for your working out.

cold drinks

2 marks

14 During the week after this survey, the weather was much hotter.

How do you think the bar chart would be different at the end of the hotter week?

Use this box to explain your answer.

2 marks

Y3: s-A

Page Total

Your class are carrying out a survey to decide where to go on the class trip. The choice is between:

a museum   a zoo   a farm   the seaside

15 Which of the following would be the best way to present the information from the class trip survey?

Circle your answer.

line graph   tally chart

Venn diagram   Carroll diagram

2 marks

End of Test

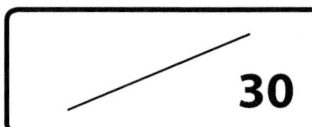
Page Total

TEST TOTAL

30

PERCENTAGE SCORE

%

Y3: s-A

Mathematics Assessment: NUMBER - Number and place value

Name .... Class .... Date ....

1 Complete the number patterns below.

a 0 ☐ 8 12 16 ☐

b 0 50 100 ☐ 200 ☐

c 0 8 16 ☐ ☐ 40

2 marks

2 Oliver is counting forward in tens. He starts at **96**, then counts on **3** more tens.

What number does he count up to? ☐

2 marks

3 Ayesha is counting backwards in hundreds. She starts at **864**, then counts back **3** more hundreds.

What number does she count back to? ☐

2 marks

4 Complete the following. Work out the answers in your head.

a 34 + 10 = ☐  **d** 386 + 100 = ☐

b 57 - 10 = ☐  **e** 829 - 100 = ☐

c 432 + 10 = ☐ **f** 176 - 100 = ☐

2 marks

Page Total ◯

5 Complete the following.

a) What is the value of the digit **5** in the number **532**?

b) What is the value of the digit **9** in the number **329**?

c) What is the value of the digit **4** in the number **348**?

2 marks

6 Put the following numbers in order of size, starting with the smallest.

	smallest		largest

a) 84   26   17

b) 358   167   528

c) 718   817   178

2 marks

7 Partition **458** in different ways by filling in the boxes below.

a) 458 = [400] + [50] + [   ]

b) 458 = [400] + [   ] + [18]

c) 458 = [200] + [   ] + [8]

2 marks

Page Total

8 Match the words to the correct figures. One has been done for you.

a fourteen   49

b six ◄────────────────┐   14

c forty nine   └────────► 6

d seventy four   432

e four hundred and thirty two   28

f twenty eight   74

---

9 Write the following numbers in words. For example, **342** would be 'three hundred and forty two'.

a 56 ....

b 186 ....

c 758 ....

d 304 ....

Page Total

10 Fill in the missing numbers to complete the number statements below.

a   18   +   ☐   =   27

b   ☐8   +   9   =   37

c   3☐   +   9   =   47

2 marks

11 Jack puts **300 grams** of sugar into a bowl. He then adds another **8** tablespoons of sugar, each containing **10 grams**.

How many grams of sugar are in the bowl now?

Show your working out in this this box.

grams

2 marks

Y3: npv-B

Page Total

12 Look at the *pattern* in the calculations below.

a What is the next answer in the pattern?

$$194 + 100 = 294$$

$$194 + 300 = 494$$

$$194 + 500 = 694$$

$$194 + 700 = \boxed{}$$

b Explain how the pattern helps you to answer the question.
Use the box below.

2 marks

13 Add together the value of the digit **4** in the number **427** to the value of the digit **6** in the number **369**.

Show your working out in this this box.

2 marks

Page Total

14 Mr Smith saved up **784** pound coins in a big bottle. He emptied the bottle and gave **£300** to Mrs Smith, **£10** to Lewis and **£10** to Olivia.

How much did Mr Smith have left?

Show your working out in this this box.

£

2 marks

15 Chloe has a secret number. It has **2** digits and it is a multiple of **8**. The digits add up to **11**.

What is Chloe's number?

2 marks

End of Test

Page Total

TEST TOTAL

30

PERCENTAGE SCORE

%

Y3: npv-B

Mathematics Assessment: NUMBER - Addition and subtraction

Name.. Class........................ Date.......................

---

1 Complete the following. Use a *mental* method that you know.

a   46 + 3   = ☐   d   38 - 5   = ☐

b   9 + 64   = ☐   e   70 - 9   = ☐

c   8 + 76   = ☐   f   84 - 6   = ☐

2 marks

---

2 Complete the following. Use a *mental* method that you know.

a   33 + 26   = ☐   c   36 + 47   = ☐

b   87 - 36   = ☐   d   190 - 18   = ☐

2 marks

---

3 Compete the following. Use a *mental* method that you know.

a   362 + 4   = ☐   d   786 - 5   = ☐

b   739 + 1   = ☐   e   870 - 1   = ☐

c   548 + 9   = ☐   f   474 - 5   = ☐

2 marks

Y3: as-B

Page Total ○

4 Compete the following. Use a *mental* method that you know.

a $235 + 30 = \boxed{}$ **d** $586 - 30 = \boxed{}$

b $746 + 20 = \boxed{}$ **e** $356 - 20 = \boxed{}$

c $548 + 50 = \boxed{}$ **f** $867 - 60 = \boxed{}$

2 marks

---

5 Complete the following. Use a *mental* method that you know.

a $367 + 200 = \boxed{}$ **d** $765 - 200 = \boxed{}$

b $485 + 400 = \boxed{}$ **e** $695 - 100 = \boxed{}$

c $846 + 200 = \boxed{}$ **f** $976 - 600 = \boxed{}$

2 marks

---

6 Use a *written* method of column addition to solve the following.

a $343 + 28 = \boxed{}$ **b** $457 + 364 = \boxed{}$

Set out your calculations in this box.

2 marks

7 Use a **written** method of column subtraction to solve the following.

a 86 - 49 = [ ]   **b** 744 - 467 = [ ]

Set out your calculations in this box.

---

8 Use a **written** method of column addition to solve the following.

a 7 + 43 + 568 = [ ]   **b** 94 + 656 + 19 = [ ]

Set out your calculations in this box.

Y3: as-B

Page Total ( )

9 Tariq wants to estimate the answer to **42 + 78**.

Circle the sum which is the best estimation.

$$40 + 70 \qquad 40 + 80 \qquad 50 + 80$$

2 marks

---

10 Holly thought that **438 + 396 = 834**.

Fill in the boxes below to show a different number statement that she could use to check her calculation.

$$\boxed{} \quad - \quad 396 \quad = \quad \boxed{}$$

2 marks

---

11 Complete the number statements below by putting one digit in each box. An example is done for you.

example $\boxed{1}\ \boxed{8} - \boxed{5} = 13$

a $\boxed{}\boxed{} - \boxed{} = 14$

b $\boxed{}\boxed{} - \boxed{} = 16$

c $\boxed{}\boxed{} - \boxed{} = 18$

2 marks

Y3: as-B

4

Page Total

12 **38 + 38 = 76.** Explain how this fact helps you know that **38 + 39 = 77**.

Use this box to explain.

---

13 Add the value of the digit **6** in the number **368** to the value of the digit **7** in the number **759**. Use the boxes below.

☐ + ☐ = ☐

---

14 Dominic builds his lego tower **143 cm** tall.
After a rest, he adds another **6 cm** to the height of his tower.
Tyler builds a tower that is **110 cm** tall.

How much taller is Dominic's tower than Tyler's?

Show your working out in this box.

cm

Y3: as-B

15 Leoni has a one litre bottle of orange juice. She pours two glasses of orange juice from the bottle. One glass has **260 ml** of orange juice and the other has **340 ml** of orange juice.

How much orange juice is left *in the bottle?*

Show your working out in this box.

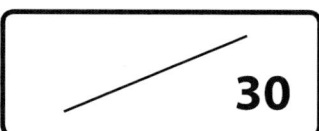

ml

2 marks

End of Test

Page Total

TEST TOTAL

30

PERCENTAGE SCORE

%

Mathematics Assessment: NUMBER - Multiplication and division

Name... Class........................ Date........................

1 Complete the following as quickly as you can.

a 3×3 = ☐   d $36 \div 3$ = ☐

b 8×3 = ☐   e $6 \div 3$ = ☐

c 9×3 = ☐   f $30 \div 3$ = ☐

2 marks

2 Complete the following as quickly as you can.

a 6×4 = ☐   d $44 \div 4$ = ☐

b 8×4 = ☐   e $12 \div 4$ = ☐

c 12×4 = ☐   f $36 \div 4$ = ☐

2 marks

3 Complete the following as quickly as you can.

a 8×8 = ☐   d $96 \div 8$ = ☐

b 6×8 = ☐   e $40 \div 8$ = ☐

c 11×8 = ☐   f $80 \div 8$ = ☐

2 marks

Y3: md-B

Page Total ◯

4 Complete the pattern below.

a

$$8 \times 2 = 16$$

$$8 \times 4 = 32$$

$$8 \times 8 = \boxed{}$$

b Imagine that the **8** times tables has been banned.

How can you work out **8 x 8** if you know that **8 x 4 = 32**?

Use this box to explain.

2 marks

5 Complete the following. Use a *mental* method that you know.

a $33 \times 3 = \boxed{}$

d $96 \div 3 = \boxed{}$

b $42 \times 4 = \boxed{}$

e $48 \div 4 = \boxed{}$

c $71 \times 8 = \boxed{}$

f $96 \div 8 = \boxed{}$

2 marks

Page Total

6 Fill in the missing numbers.

a   4   x   3   x   8   =   ☐

b   8   x   ☐   x   3   =   96

2 marks

---

7 Fill in the missing number.

5   x   5   x   8   =   200

so   ☐   x   8   =   200

2 marks

---

8 *Circle* the number statement which could help you solve **90 ÷ 30**.

$3 \div 9 = 3$ $9 \times 3 = 27$ $9 \div 3 = 3$

2 marks

---

9 Use a *written* method of multiplication to solve the following.

a 28 x 4   =   ☐   **b** 76 x 8   =   ☐

Set out your calculations in this box.

2 marks

Page Total

10 Use a **written** method of division to solve the following.

a 96 ÷ 3 = ☐   **b** 924 ÷ 4 = ☐

Set out your calculations in this box.

---

11 A rounders bat measures **67 cm**.

Use a **written** method of **multiplication** to find the length of **3** rounders bats placed end to end.

Show your working out in this box.

cm

12 A box of chocolates has **78** chocolates in **3** layers.

Use a **written** method of **division** to find how many chocolates are in each layer.

Show your working out in this box.

| chocolates |

2 marks

13 Amelia made a model bird house that was **87 cm** tall.
Amelia's dad made the real bird house three times as tall as Amelia's.

How tall was Amelia's dad's bird house?

Show your working out in this box.

| cm |

2 marks

Y3: md-B

Page Total

14 Levi has **7** different t-shirts and **4** different pairs of jeans.

How many different outfits can Levi make?

Show your working out in this box.

outfits

2 marks

15 A taxi can carry **4** people.

How many taxis would be needed to take **568** people to a football match?

Show your working out in this box.

taxis

2 marks

End of Test

TEST TOTAL

PERCENTAGE SCORE

/ 30

%

Y3: md-B

Mathematics Assessment: NUMBER - Fractions

Name.. Class......................... Date.........................

1 Complete the patterns by writing the missing fractions in the boxes.

a

| $\dfrac{5}{10}$ | $\dfrac{6}{10}$ | $\dfrac{7}{10}$ | $\dfrac{\quad}{\quad}$ | $\dfrac{9}{10}$ |

b

| $\dfrac{6}{10}$ | $\dfrac{\quad}{\quad}$ | $\dfrac{4}{10}$ | $\dfrac{3}{10}$ | $\dfrac{2}{10}$ |

2 marks

---

2 Look at the shape below.

a How many tenths are shaded?

| tenths |

b Now complete the shading on the shape so that **seven tenths** of the shape are shaded.

2 marks

Y3: f-B

Page Total

3 Match the fractions to the decimals. One has been done for you.

a   0.4

b   0.9

c   0.2

d   0.5

$$\frac{5}{10}$$

$$\frac{2}{10}$$

$$\frac{4}{10}$$

$$\frac{9}{10}$$

2 marks

---

4 Complete the following.

a $4 \div 10 =$ ☐

b $8 \div 10 =$ ☐

c $2 \div 10 =$ ☐

Remember,
6 divided by
10 is 0.6

2 marks

Y3: f-B

2

Page Total

5 What fraction of the buttons is in the ring?

Circle your answer.

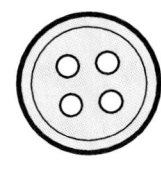
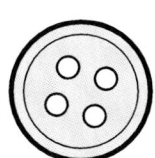
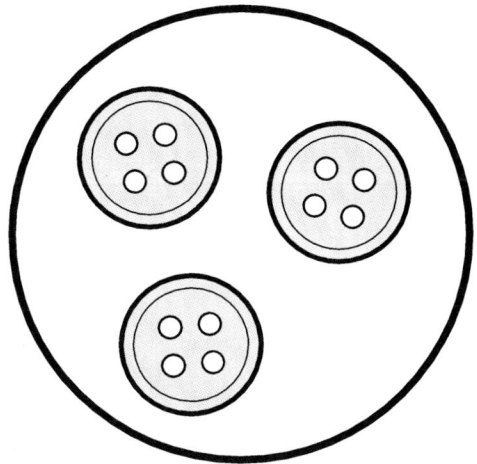

$$\frac{3}{5} \qquad \frac{2}{5}$$

$$\frac{5}{6} \qquad \frac{1}{5}$$

2 marks

---

6 Draw an arrow (↓) pointing to **4½** on the number line.

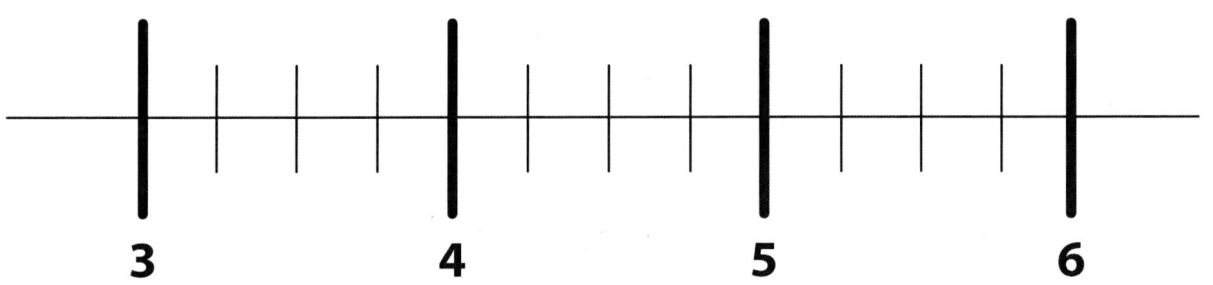

2 marks

Page Total

7 Look at Ava's apple pie. She has eaten some.

How much does she **have left?**

Write your answer as a **fraction**.

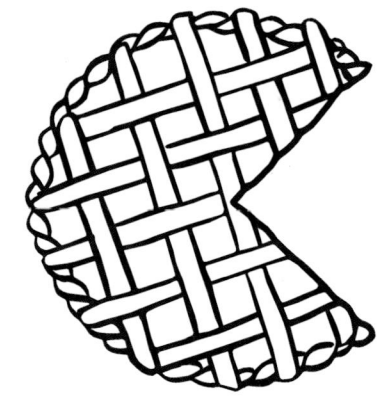

2 marks

---

8 Which is more? Tick (✓) the box.

| $\dfrac{1}{4}$ of 20 litres | **or** | $\dfrac{1}{2}$ of 12 litres |

2 marks

---

9 Complete the following.

a $\dfrac{1}{4}$ of 24 = ☐

b $\dfrac{1}{3}$ of 27 = ☐

2 marks

Y3: f-B

Page Total

10 Match the equal fractions. One has been done for you.

a) $\dfrac{1}{2}$

b) $\dfrac{1}{3}$

c) $\dfrac{1}{4}$

d) $\dfrac{1}{5}$

$\dfrac{2}{6}$

$\dfrac{2}{4}$

$\dfrac{2}{10}$

$\dfrac{2}{8}$

11 Shade some of shape **B** to match shape **A**.

A

B

Page Total

12 Complete the following.

a $\dfrac{1}{4} + \dfrac{2}{4} = \boxed{}$

b $\dfrac{5}{9} + \dfrac{1}{9} = \boxed{}$

2 marks

---

13 Complete the following.

a $\dfrac{4}{5} - \dfrac{2}{5} = \boxed{}$

b $\dfrac{7}{8} - \dfrac{5}{8} = \boxed{}$

2 marks

---

14 Put these fractions in order of size, starting with the smallest.

a $\dfrac{6}{7}$ $\dfrac{1}{7}$ $\dfrac{3}{7}$ $\dfrac{5}{7}$

$\boxed{}$ $\boxed{}$ $\boxed{}$ $\boxed{}$

smallest   **largest**

b $\dfrac{1}{3}$ $\dfrac{1}{5}$ $\dfrac{1}{10}$ $\dfrac{1}{8}$

$\boxed{}$ $\boxed{}$ $\boxed{}$ $\boxed{}$

smallest   **largest**

2 marks

Page Total

15 On Friday, Finlay ate **three sevenths** of his raspberry pie.

On Saturday, he ate another $\frac{2}{7}$ of his pie.

How much did he eat on Friday and Saturday altogether?

Use this box if you need to do any working out.

He ate [——] of his pie

on Friday and Saturday altogether.

2 marks

End of Test

Y3: f-B

7

Page Total ◯

TEST TOTAL

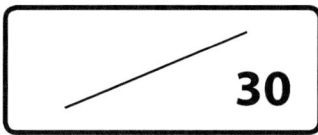

30

PERCENTAGE SCORE

%

Mathematics Assessment: MEASUREMENT

Name .... Class .... Date ....

1 What length is the arrow showing?

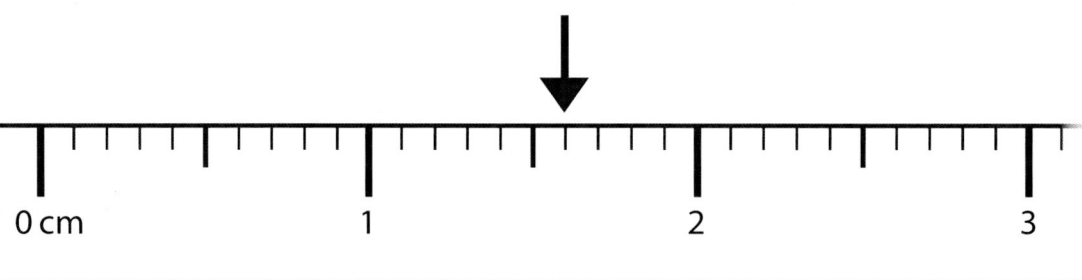

| _____ cm _____ mm |

2 marks

2 What measurement is shown on the scales?

| kg |

2 marks

3 Eli is **1 m 26 cm** tall and Max is **138 cm** tall. Who is taller?

Use this box if you need to do any working out.

| is taller |

2 marks

4 How much water is in the measuring jug?

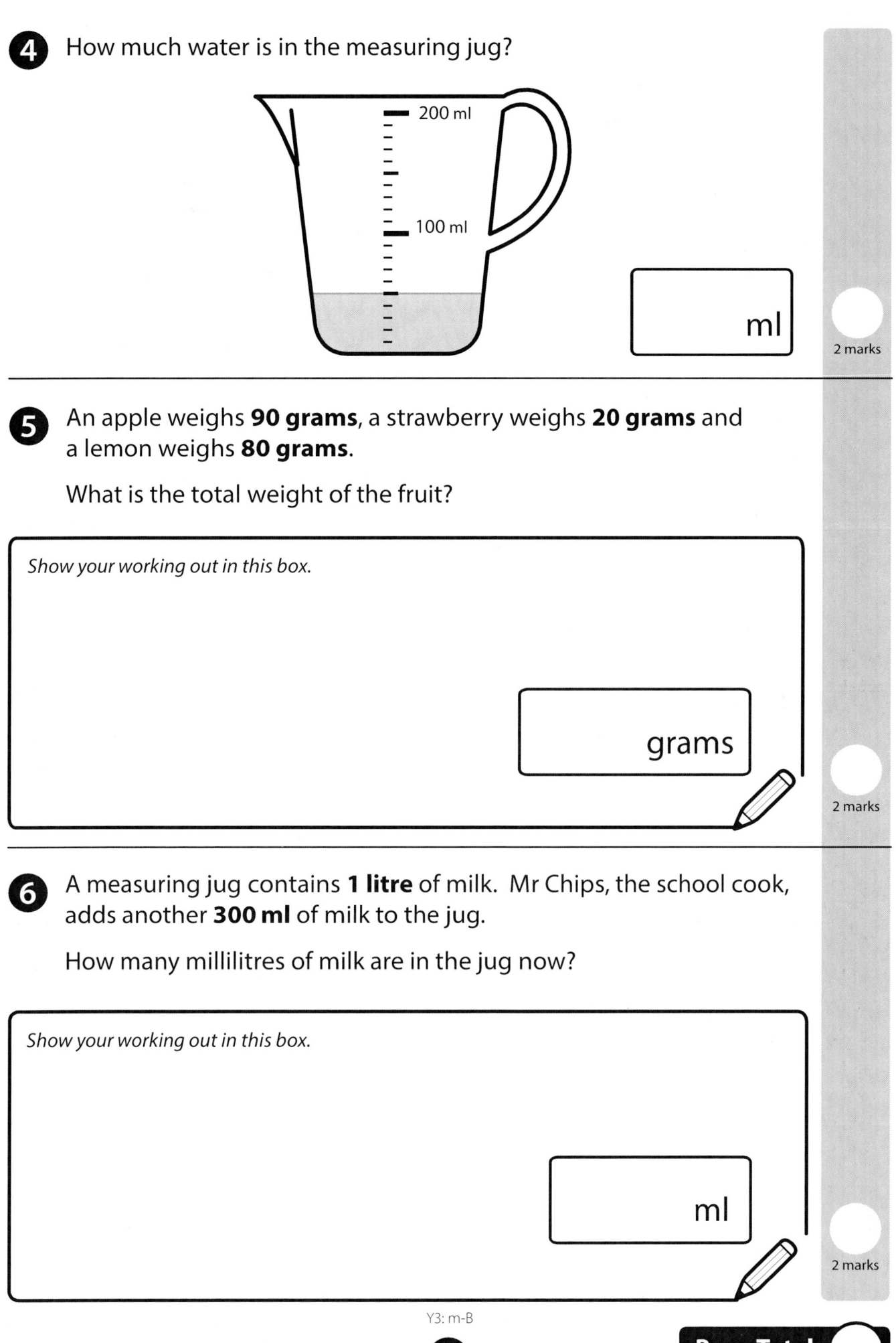

200 ml

100 ml

ml

2 marks

5 An apple weighs **90 grams**, a strawberry weighs **20 grams** and a lemon weighs **80 grams**.

What is the total weight of the fruit?

Show your working out in this box.

grams

2 marks

6 A measuring jug contains **1 litre** of milk. Mr Chips, the school cook, adds another **300 ml** of milk to the jug.

How many millilitres of milk are in the jug now?

Show your working out in this box.

ml

2 marks

Y3: m-B

Page Total

7 Use your ruler to measure the **perimeter** of the rectangle below.

The perimeter measures ⬚ cm

---

8 In a newsagents, a pad of paper costs **£1.55** and a pen costs **£1.00**.

If James buys a pad of paper and a pen, how much change will he get from **£5.00**?

Show your working out in this box.

£ ⬚

---

9 Ellie has **seven £1** coins, **one 50p** coin and **four 10p** coins.

How much does she have altogether?

Show your working out in this box.

£ ⬚

Page Total ⬚

10 What time is it?

Write your answers in the boxes below the clocks.

a
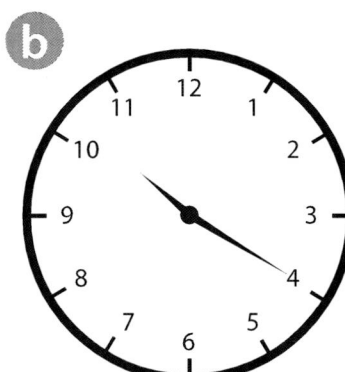

b
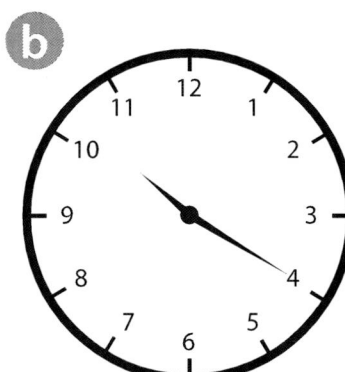

c
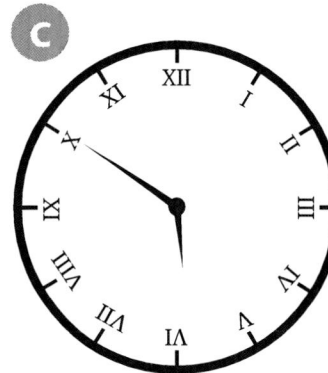

2 marks

---

11 Draw the times shown on the clocks below.

a
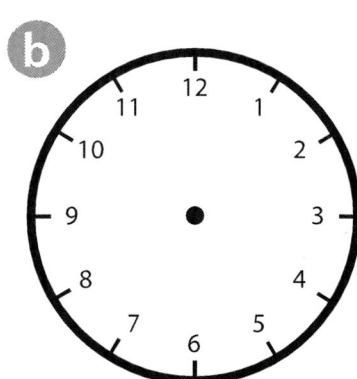

b

c
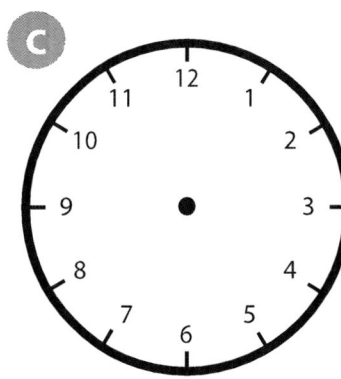

2 o'clock	6:15 am	19:00

2 marks

Y3: m-B

Page Total

12 Mila started running at the time shown on clock **A.**

She stopped at the time shown on clock **B.**

Estimate how many minutes she ran for.

A

B

minutes

---

13 Write **TRUE (T)** or **FALSE (F)** after these statements.

a When it's morning, it's **am**.

b When it's morning, it's **pm**.

c When it's noon, it will be midnight in 12 hours.

Page Total

14 Find the matching pairs below. Join them with a line. One has been done for you.

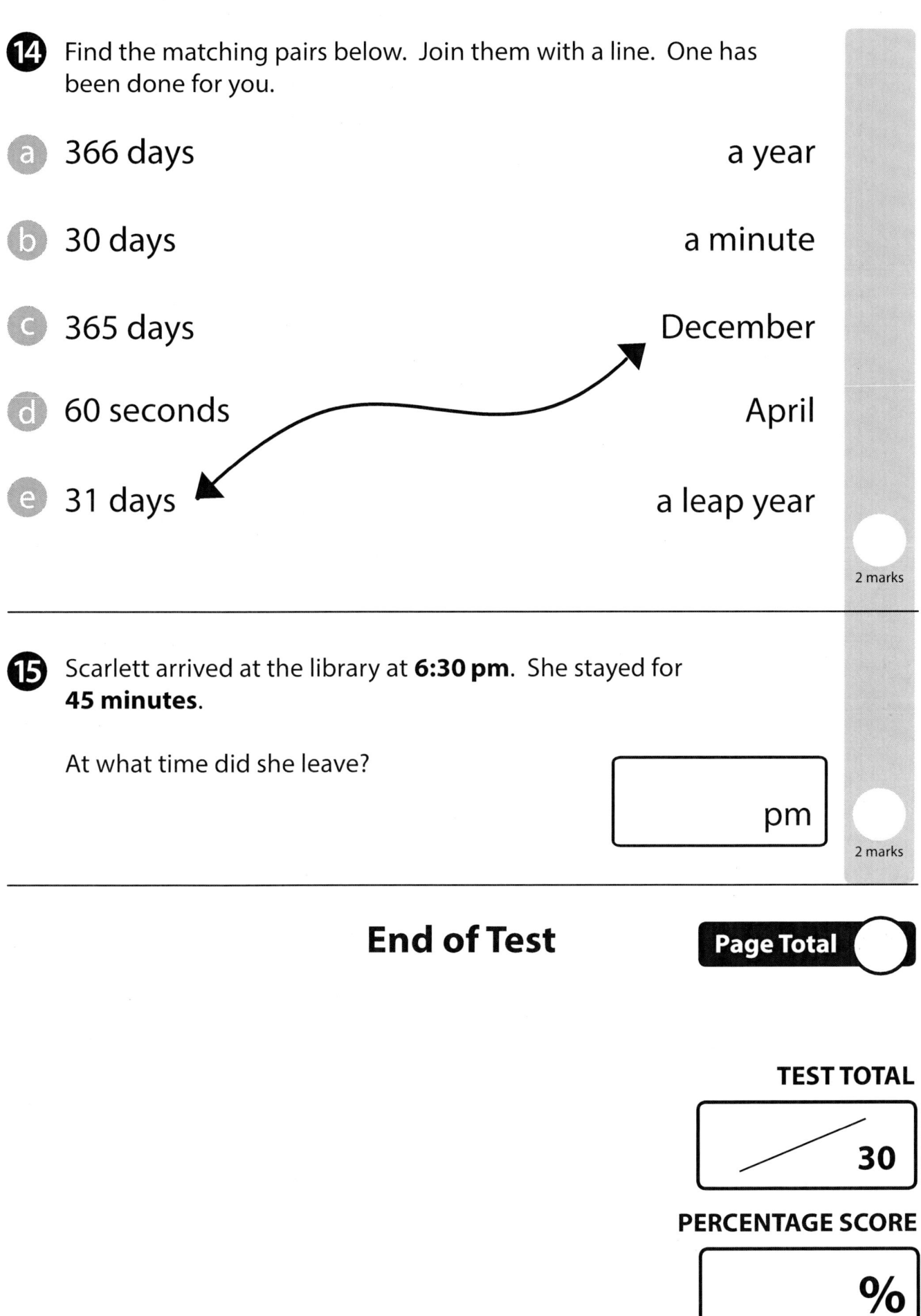

a 366 days   a year

b 30 days   a minute

c 365 days   December

d 60 seconds   April

e 31 days   a leap year

---

15 Scarlett arrived at the library at **6:30 pm**. She stayed for **45 minutes**.

At what time did she leave?

pm

End of Test

Page Total

TEST TOTAL

30

PERCENTAGE SCORE

%

Mathematics Assessment: GEOMETRY - Properties of shapes

Name.. Class........................ Date........................

1 Use your ruler to draw a rectangle in the space below.

2 marks

2 Mustapha drew a line **7.5 cm** long as one side of his rectangle. He then decided to round the length of the line up to the next whole number.

How long was Mustapha's line after rounding?

 cm

2 marks

3 Match the 3D shapes to their names. One has been done for you.

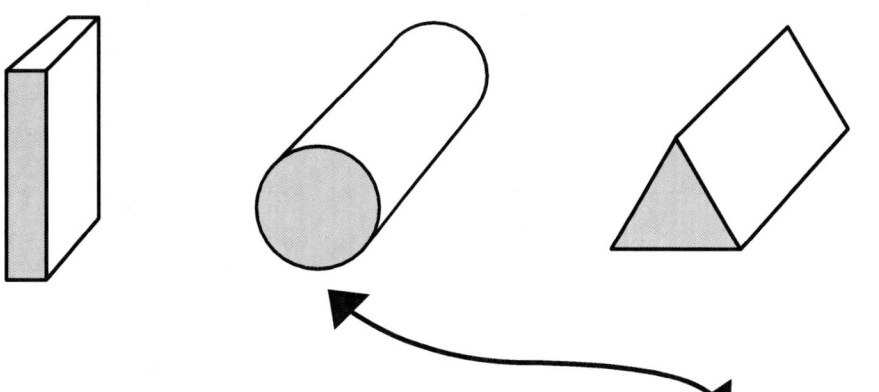

a prism   b cube   c cylinder   d cuboid

2 marks

Y3: g-B

Page Total

4 Match the 2D or 3D shapes to their description. One has been done for you.

a pentagon

b prism

c circle

d sphere

e square

a 2D shape with **4** equal sides and **4** equal angles

a 3D shape that is round like a football

a 2D shape with **5** sides, **5** angles and **5** lines of symmetry

a 3D shape with **2** triangular faces and **3** rectangular faces

a 2D shape with one curved side and no angles

2 marks

Y3: g-B

2

Page Total

5 Choose **one** word from the brackets to complete the sentence below.

Number of _____ is a property of shapes.

(angles, lengths, widths)

2 marks

6 Choose **one** word from the brackets to complete the sentence below.

_____ show amounts of turn.

(Sides, Angles, Corners)

2 marks

7 Camillla is facing west. She then turns to face east.

How many **right angles** has she turned through?

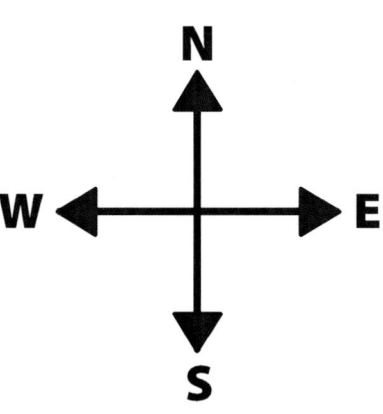

right angles

2 marks

Y3: g-B

Page Total

8 Look at the shape below. Put a tick (✔) next to the right angle.

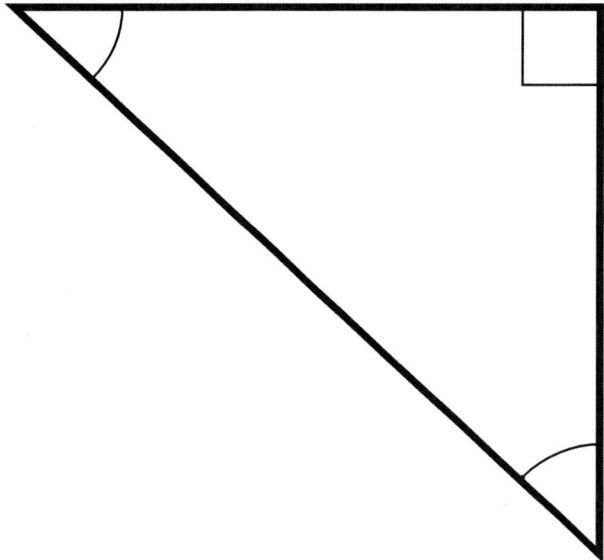

9 Write **TRUE (T)** or **FALSE (F)** after these statements.

a Three right angles make a half-turn.

b One right angle makes a quarter-turn.

c Four right angles make a complete turn.

d Two right angles make a half-turn.

Y3: g-B

Page Total

10 Are the angles below greater than or less than a right angle?

Write '**greater**' or '**less**' in the boxes.

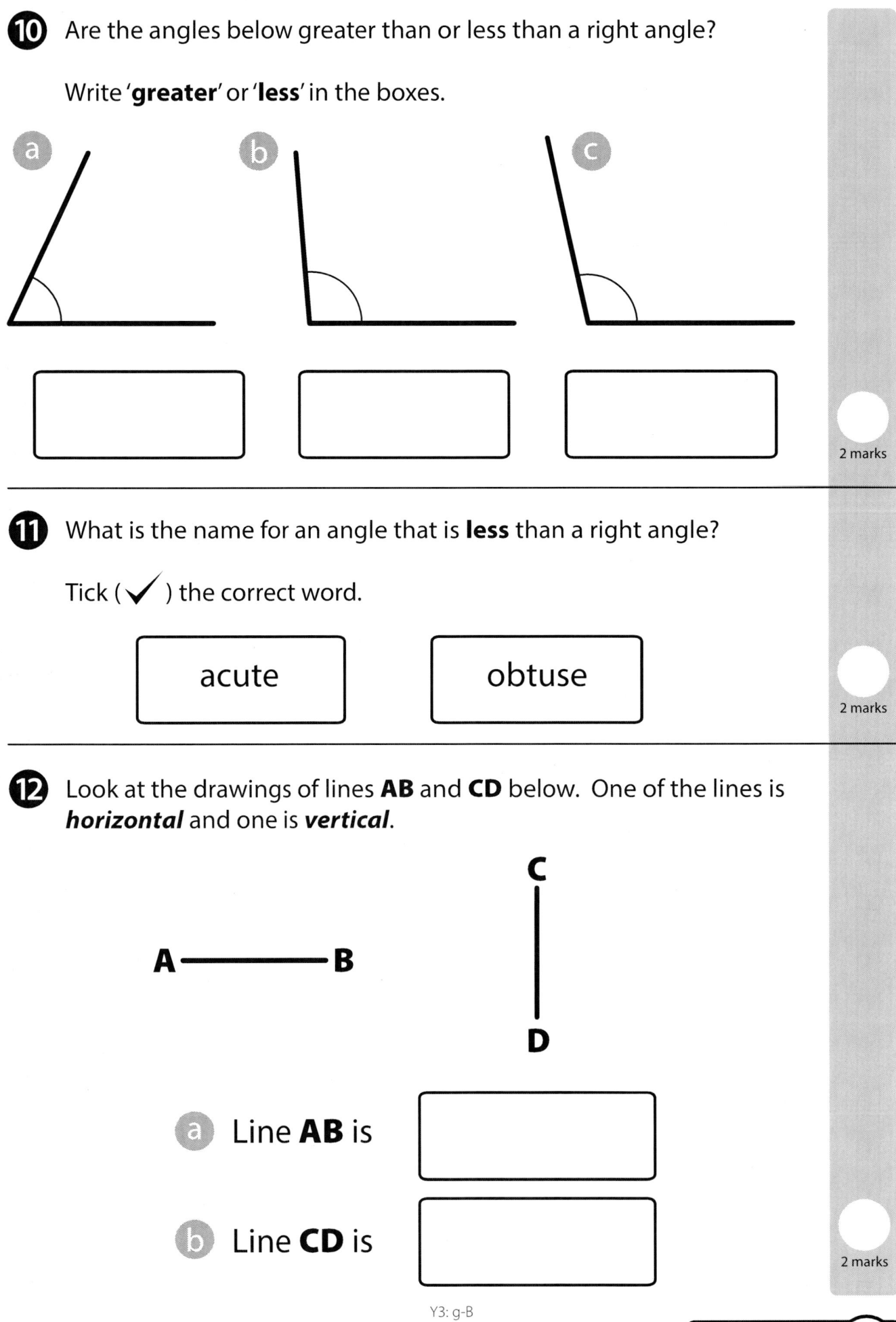

a

b

c

2 marks

---

11 What is the name for an angle that is **less** than a right angle?

Tick (✓) the correct word.

acute	obtuse

2 marks

---

12 Look at the drawings of lines **AB** and **CD** below. One of the lines is *horizontal* and one is *vertical*.

A ——— B

C
|
|
D

a Line **AB** is

b Line **CD** is

2 marks

Page Total

13 In the space below, use your ruler to draw a line that is *perpendicular* to line **AB**.

A ——————————————————————— B

2 marks

14 In the space below, use your ruler to draw a line that is *parallel* to line **AB**.

A ——————————————————————— B

2 marks

Page Total

15 Write **TRUE (T)** or **FALSE (F)** after these statements.

a Perpendicular lines are always the same distance apart.

☐

b Parallel lines are always the same distance apart.

☐

c A horizontal line goes straight up and down.

☐

d A vertical line goes straight up and down.

☐

2 marks

End of Test

Page Total ◯

TEST TOTAL

⟋ 30

PERCENTAGE SCORE

%

Y3: g-B

Mathematics Assessment: STATISTICS

Name.. Class........................ Date........................

Look at the bar chart below.

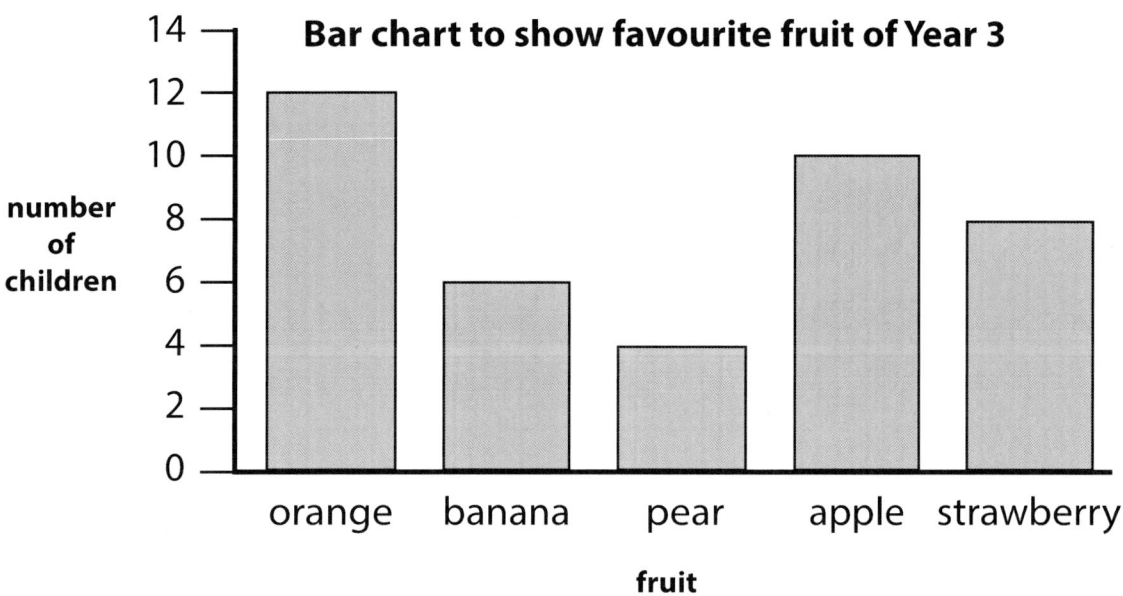

Bar chart to show favourite fruit of Year 3

number of children

fruit

Now answer these questions.

1 What is the most popular fruit in Year 3?

2 marks

2 How many more people like oranges than bananas?

people

2 marks

3 If **3** people changed their mind and said they liked pears and not bananas, how many more people would like pears than bananas?

people

2 marks

Page Total

Look at the tally chart below.

Animals in the zoo

Animal	Tally
penguins	ЖЖ ЖЖ ||
tigers	|||||
bears	ЖЖ
camels	ЖЖ ||||

Now answer these questions.

4 How many bears are in the zoo?

[ ] bears

2 marks

5 How many more penguins are there than tigers?

[ ]

2 marks

6 Zoe says, "There are more penguins than there are tigers and camels put together."

Is that true? (Yes or No)

[ ]

Use this box to explain how you know.

2 marks

Y3: s-B

2

Page Total ○

Look at the pictogram below.

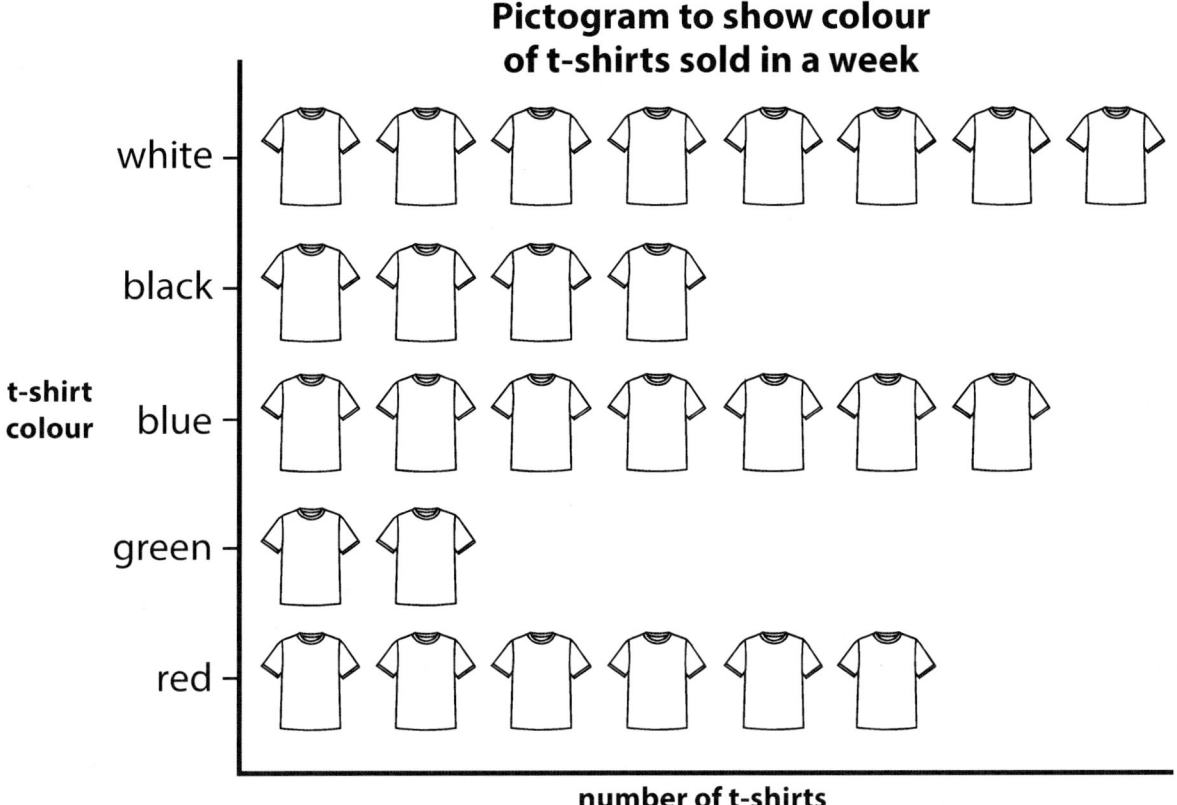

Pictogram to show colour of t-shirts sold in a week

t-shirt colour:
- white
- black
- blue
- green
- red

number of t-shirts

Now answer these questions.

7 How many white and blue t-shirts are sold altogether?

8 How many more red t-shirts are sold than green t-shirts?

9 During the next week, white, blue and red t-shirts sold the same amount as shown on the pictogram. Green sold **4** more and black sold **2** more.

Draw more t-shirts on the pictogram to show this information.

Y3: s-B

Page Total

Look at the frequency table below.

Name	Number of children with this name in the school
Chloe	9
Tom	5
Olivia	6
Aiden	13
Emily	11

Now answer these questions.

10 How many children are called Emily?

children

2 marks

11 How many more children are called Aiden than are called Tom?

children

2 marks

12 Using the information in the table, write a question that you could ask about the names of children in the school.

Write your question in this box.

2 marks

Page Total

13 Look at the bar chart below.

a Firstly, draw in a bar to show that **8** ice creams were sold on Thursday.

b Now work out how many ice creams were sold all week.

Use this box for your working out.

| ice creams |

2 marks

14 During the week after this survey, the weather was much colder.

How do you think the bar chart would be different at the end of the colder week?

Use this box to explain your answer.

2 marks

Y3: s-B

Page Total

Your class are carrying out a survey to find out what kind of books children like to read. The choice is between:

animals   hobbies   stories   information

15 Which of the following would be the best way to present the information from the favourite book survey?

Circle your answer.

Carroll diagram   Venn diagram

tally chart   line graph

2 marks

End of Test

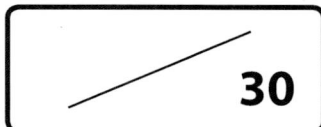 Page Total

TEST TOTAL

/ 30

PERCENTAGE SCORE

%

Y3: s-B

Mathematics Assessment: NUMBER - Number and place value

Name .... Class .... Date ....

1 Complete the number patterns below.

a   0   4   [   ]   [   ]   16   20

b   0   [   ]   100   150   200   [   ]

c   0   8   [   ]   24   32   [   ]

2 marks

2 Eli is counting forward in tens. He starts at **74**, then counts on **3** more tens.

What number does he count up to?   [   ]

2 marks

3 Emma is counting backwards in hundreds. She starts at **736**, then counts back **3** more hundreds.

What number does she count back to?   [   ]

2 marks

4 Complete the following. Work out the answers in your head.

a 46 + 10 = [   ]   **d** 256 + 100 = [   ]

b 38 - 10 = [   ]   **e** 494 - 100 = [   ]

c 565 + 10 = [   ]   **f** 187 - 100 = [   ]

2 marks

Page Total ◯

5 Complete the following.

a) What is the value of the digit **7** in the number **724**? ____

b) What is the value of the digit **2** in the number **482**? ____

c) What is the value of the digit **6** in the number **365**? ____

2 marks

---

6 Put the following numbers in order of size, starting with the smallest.

	smallest		largest
a) 47 82 31	____	____	____
b) 397 543 248	____	____	____
c) 615 516 156	____	____	____

2 marks

---

7 Partition **559** in different ways by filling in the boxes below.

a) 559 = [500] + [50] + [____]

b) 559 = [500] + [____] + [19]

c) 559 = [200] + [____] + [9]

2 marks

Y3: npv-C

2

Page Total

8 Match the words to the correct figures. One has been done for you.

a eighteen   97

b seven   71

c seventy one   18

d ninety seven   364

e three hundred
   and sixty four   30

f thirty   7

2 marks

---

9 Write the following numbers in words. For example, **562** would be 'five hundred and sixty two'.

a 86 ....

b 143 ....

c 649 ....

d 806 ....

2 marks

Y3: npv-C

Page Total

10 Fill in the missing numbers to complete the number statements below.

a 15 + [6] = 21

b [ ]5 + 6 = 31

c 3[ ] + 6 = 41

2 marks

11 Ryan puts **400 grams** of sand into his seaside bucket. He then adds another **6** scoops of sand, each containing **10 grams**.

How many grams of sand are in the bucket now?

Show your working out in this this box.

grams

2 marks

12 Look at the *pattern* in the calculations below.

a What is the next answer in the pattern?

187 + 200 = 387

187 + 400 = 587

187 + 600 = 787

187 + 800 = ☐

b Explain how the pattern helps you to answer the question. Use the box below.

2 marks

---

13 Add together the value of the digit **7** in the number **724** to the value of the digit **4** in the number **349**.

Show your working out in this this box.

2 marks

Page Total

14 Mrs Jackson saved up **842** pound coins in a giant piggy bank. She emptied the piggy bank and gave **£400** to Mr Jackson, **£10** to Izzie and **£10** to William.

How much did Mrs Jackson have left?

Show your working out in this this box.

£

15 Connor has a secret number. It has **2** digits and it is a multiple of **8**. The digits add up to **15**.

What is Connor's number?

End of Test

Page Total

TEST TOTAL

30

PERCENTAGE SCORE

%

Mathematics Assessment: NUMBER - Addition and subtraction

Name.. Class......................... Date.........................

1 Complete the following. Use a *mental* method that you know.

a $32 + 4 \ = \ \boxed{}$

b $7 + 46 \ = \ \boxed{}$

c $6 + 68 \ = \ \boxed{}$

d $47 - 4 \ = \ \boxed{}$

e $90 - 9 \ = \ \boxed{}$

f $76 - 8 \ = \ \boxed{}$

2 marks

2 Complete the following. Use a *mental* method that you know.

a $42 + 37 \ = \ \boxed{}$

b $69 - 27 \ = \ \boxed{}$

c $29 + 67 \ = \ \boxed{}$

d $170 - 19 \ = \ \boxed{}$

2 marks

3 Compete the following. Use a *mental* method that you know.

a $624 + 5 \ = \ \boxed{}$

b $359 + 1 \ = \ \boxed{}$

c $467 + 9 \ = \ \boxed{}$

d $487 - 3 \ = \ \boxed{}$

e $940 - 1 \ = \ \boxed{}$

f $875 - 6 \ = \ \boxed{}$

2 marks

Y3: as-C

Page Total

4 Compete the following. Use a *mental* method that you know.

a 549 + 10 = ☐   **d** 693 - 40 = ☐

b 627 + 30 = ☐   **e** 248 - 20 = ☐

c 738 + 60 = ☐   **f** 494 - 90 = ☐

2 marks

5 Complete the following. Use a *mental* method that you know.

a 326 + 300 = ☐   **d** 843 - 300 = ☐

b 578 + 100 = ☐   **e** 586 - 200 = ☐

c 624 + 400 = ☐   **f** 863 - 500 = ☐

2 marks

6 Use a *written* method of column addition to solve the following.

a 419 + 46 = ☐   **b** 257 + 559 = ☐

Set out your calculations in this box.

2 marks

Y3: as-C

Page Total ◯

7 Use a *written* method of column subtraction to solve the following.

a 72 - 56 = [ ]   **b** 536 - 269 = [ ]

Set out your calculations in this box.

---

8 Use a *written* method of column addition to solve the following.

a 48 + 8 + 361 = [ ]   **b** 487 + 16 + 83 = [ ]

Set out your calculations in this box.

Y3: as-C

Page Total ( )

9 Elliot wants to estimate the answer to **33 + 68**.

Circle the sum which is the best estimation.

$$30 + 70 \qquad\qquad 40 + 70 \qquad\qquad 30 + 60$$

2 marks

---

10 Bella thought that **297 + 364 = 661**.

Fill in the boxes below to show a different number statement that she could use to check her calculation.

$$\boxed{} \quad - \quad 364 \quad = \quad \boxed{}$$

2 marks

---

11 Complete the number statements below by putting one digit in each box. An example is done for you.

example $\boxed{1}\;\boxed{7}\; - \;\boxed{6} = 11$

a $\boxed{}\,\boxed{}\; - \;\boxed{} = 12$

b $\boxed{}\,\boxed{}\; - \;\boxed{} = 17$

c $\boxed{}\,\boxed{}\; - \;\boxed{} = 19$

2 marks

Y3: as-C

Page Total

12 **46 + 46 = 92.** Explain how this fact helps you know that **46 + 47 = 93**.

Use this box to explain.

2 marks

---

13 Add the value of the digit **7** in the number **679** to the value of the digit **8** in the number **823**. Use the boxes below.

☐ + ☐ = ☐

2 marks

---

14 Yasmin unwinds **163 cm** from a ball of wool. Then she unwinds another **6 cm** from the ball and cuts off the whole piece of wool.

Josh unwinds **120 cm** from the ball and cuts it off.

How much longer is Yasmin's piece of wool than Josh's?

Show your working out in this box.

☐ cm

2 marks

Y3: as-C

Page Total ◯

15 Ethan has a one litre bottle of cola. He pours two glasses of cola from the bottle. One glass has **310 ml** of cola and the other has **290 ml** of cola.

How much cola is left *in the bottle?*

Show your working out in this box.

ml

2 marks

End of Test

Page Total

Mathematics Assessment: NUMBER - Multiplication and division

Name... Class........................ Date........................

1 Complete the following as quickly as you can.

a 4×3 = ☐   d $33 \div 3$ = ☐

b 7×3 = ☐   e $27 \div 3$ = ☐

c 5×3 = ☐   f $12 \div 3$ = ☐

2 marks

2 Complete the following as quickly as you can.

a 11×4 = ☐   d $16 \div 4$ = ☐

b 3×4 = ☐   e $24 \div 4$ = ☐

c 10×4 = ☐   f $4 \div 4$ = ☐

2 marks

3 Complete the following as quickly as you can.

a 9×8 = ☐   d $8 \div 8$ = ☐

b 4×8 = ☐   e $24 \div 8$ = ☐

c 12×8 = ☐   f $56 \div 8$ = ☐

2 marks

Y3: md-C

Page Total ◯

4 Complete the pattern below.

a
$$4 \times 2 = 8$$

$$4 \times 4 = 16$$

$$4 \times 8 = \boxed{}$$

b Imagine that the **8** times tables has been banned.

How can you work out **4 x 8** if you know that **4 x 4 = 16**?

Use this box to explain.

2 marks

5 Complete the following. Use a *mental* method that you know.

a 32 x 3 = ☐   d 39 ÷ 3 = ☐

b 52 x 4 = ☐   e 88 ÷ 4 = ☐

c 61 x 8 = ☐   f 96 ÷ 8 = ☐

2 marks

6 Fill in the missing numbers.

a) $8 \quad x \quad 4 \quad x \quad 3 \quad = \quad \boxed{}$

b) $3 \quad x \quad \boxed{} \quad x \quad 4 \quad = \quad 96$

2 marks

---

7 Fill in the missing number.

$5 \quad x \quad 6 \quad x \quad 7 \quad = \quad 210$

so $\quad \boxed{} \quad x \quad 7 \quad = \quad 210$

2 marks

---

8 *Circle* the number statement which could help you solve **120 ÷ 40**.

$12 \div 4 = 3 \qquad 4 \times 12 = 48 \qquad 4 \div 12 = 3$

2 marks

---

9 Use a **written** method of multiplication to solve the following.

a) $29 \times 3 \quad = \quad \boxed{}$ 　　　 b) $65 \times 8 \quad = \quad \boxed{}$

Set out your calculations in this box.

2 marks

Page Total

10 Use a **written** method of division to solve the following.

a 69 ÷ 3 = [ ]   **b** 896 ÷ 8 = [ ]

Set out your calculations in this box.

11 A railway carriage is **23 m** long.

Use a **written** method of **multiplication** to find the length of **8** railway carriages placed end to end.

Show your working out in this box.

[ ] m

Page Total

12 A car park has a total of **968** cars shared equally between **8** floors.

Use a **written** method of **division** to find how many cars are on each floor.

Show your working out in this box.

> cars

2 marks

---

13 Theo planted an apple tree that was **64 cm** tall.
After **3** years, it had grown to eight times the original size.

How tall was the tree after **3** years?

Show your working out in this box.

> cm

2 marks

Y3: md-C

14 Jaycilou has **6** different dresses and **8** different pairs of shoes. How many different outfits can Jaycilou make?

Show your working out in this box.

outfits

2 marks

15 Each cage in the petshop superstore holds **8** mice.

How many cages are needed to hold **968** mice?

Show your working out in this box.

cages

2 marks

End of Test

Page Total

TEST TOTAL

30

Y3: md-C

PERCENTAGE SCORE

%

Mathematics Assessment: NUMBER - Fractions

Name.. Class........................ Date........................

1 Complete the patterns by writing the missing fractions in the boxes.

a

$\dfrac{2}{10}$ $\dfrac{3}{10}$ $\underline{}$ $\dfrac{5}{10}$ $\dfrac{6}{10}$

b

$\underline{}$ $\dfrac{7}{10}$ $\dfrac{6}{10}$ $\dfrac{5}{10}$ $\dfrac{4}{10}$

2 marks

2 Look at the shape below.

a How many tenths are shaded?

tenths

b Now complete the shading on the shape so that **eight tenths** of the shape are shaded.

2 marks

Y3: f-C

Page Total

 Match the fractions to the decimals. One has been done for you.

a 0.3

b 0.7

c 0.6

d 0.9

$$\frac{9}{10}$$

$$\frac{3}{10}$$

$$\frac{7}{10}$$

$$\frac{6}{10}$$

2 marks

4 Complete the following.

a $3 \div 10 = \boxed{}$

b $5 \div 10 = \boxed{}$

c $1 \div 10 = \boxed{}$

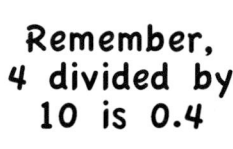

Remember, 4 divided by 10 is 0.4

2 marks

Y3: f-C

Page Total

5 What fraction of the buttons is **<u>not</u>** in the ring?

Circle your answer.

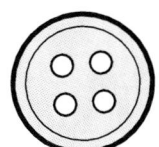 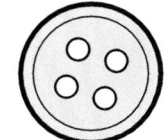

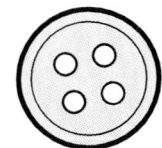

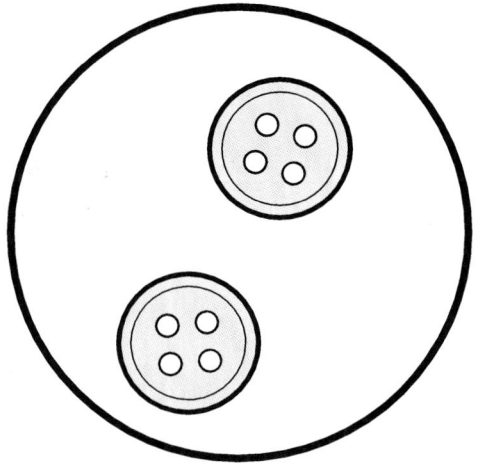

$$\frac{3}{5} \qquad \frac{2}{5}$$

$$\frac{5}{6} \qquad \frac{1}{5}$$

---

6 Draw an arrow (↓) pointing to **$3\frac{1}{2}$** on the number line.

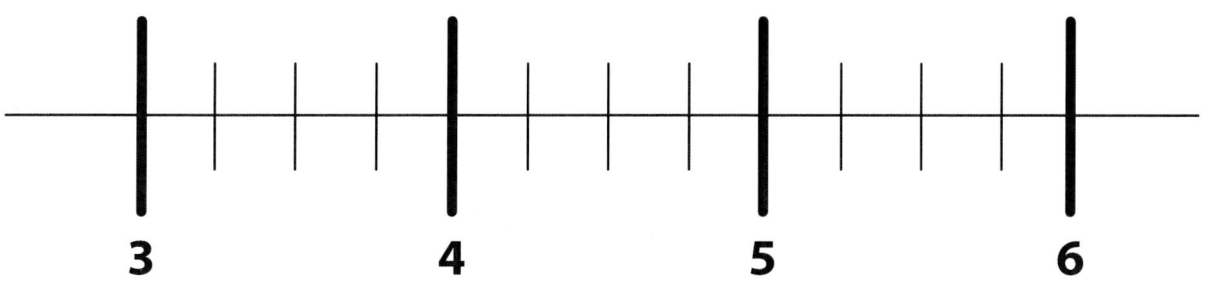

Y3: f-C

Page Total

7 Look at Henry's custard pie.

How much has he eaten? Write your answer as a *fraction*.

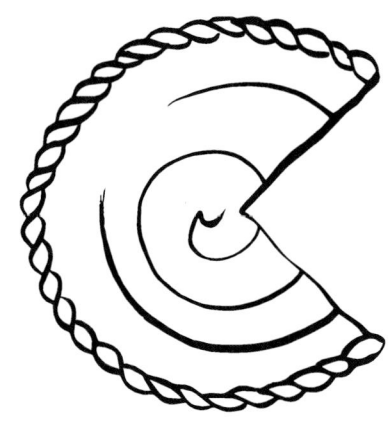

---

8 Which is more? Tick (✔) the box.

| $\frac{1}{3}$ of 27 litres | **or** | $\frac{1}{5}$ of 40 litres |

---

9 Complete the following.

a $\frac{1}{6}$ of 30 = ☐   **b** $\frac{1}{4}$ of 36 = ☐

Y3: f-C

Page Total

10 Match the equal fractions. One has been done for you.

a) $\dfrac{1}{5}$

b) $\dfrac{1}{4}$

c) $\dfrac{1}{3}$

d) $\dfrac{1}{2}$

$\dfrac{2}{4}$

$\dfrac{2}{6}$

$\dfrac{2}{10}$

$\dfrac{2}{8}$

2 marks

11 Shade some of shape **B** to match shape **A**.

A

B

2 marks

Y3: f-C

5

Page Total

12 Complete the following.

a $\dfrac{1}{6} + \dfrac{4}{6} = \boxed{}$ **b** $\dfrac{3}{8} + \dfrac{2}{8} = \boxed{}$

2 marks

13 Complete the following.

a $\dfrac{8}{9} - \dfrac{2}{9} = \boxed{}$ **b** $\dfrac{6}{7} - \dfrac{5}{7} = \boxed{}$

2 marks

14 Put these fractions in order of size, starting with the smallest.

a $\dfrac{7}{8}$ $\dfrac{3}{8}$ $\dfrac{4}{8}$ $\dfrac{1}{8}$

$\boxed{}$ $\boxed{}$ $\boxed{}$ $\boxed{}$

smallest   **largest**

b $\dfrac{1}{7}$ $\dfrac{1}{11}$ $\dfrac{1}{2}$ $\dfrac{1}{6}$

$\boxed{}$ $\boxed{}$ $\boxed{}$ $\boxed{}$

smallest   **largest**

2 marks

Y3: f-C

Page Total

15 On Monday, Mia ate **four ninths** of her chocolate bar.

On Tuesday, she ate another $\frac{2}{9}$ of her chocolate bar.

How much did she eat on Monday and Tuesday altogether?

Use this box if you need to do any working out.

She ate $\boxed{}$ of her chocolate bar

on Monday and Tuesday altogether.

2 marks

End of Test

TEST TOTAL

30

PERCENTAGE SCORE

%

Y3: f-C

Mathematics Assessment: MEASUREMENT

Name.. Class...................... Date......................

1 What length is the arrow showing?

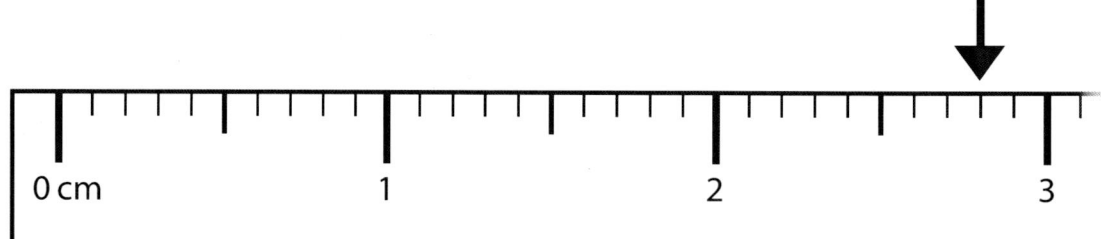

_____ cm _____ mm

2 marks

2 What measurement is shown on the scales?

_____ kg

2 marks

3 Eva is **1 m 42 cm** tall and Seb is **124 cm** tall. Who is taller?

Use this box if you need to do any working out.

_____ is taller

2 marks

Y3: m-C

Page Total

4 How much water is in the measuring jug?

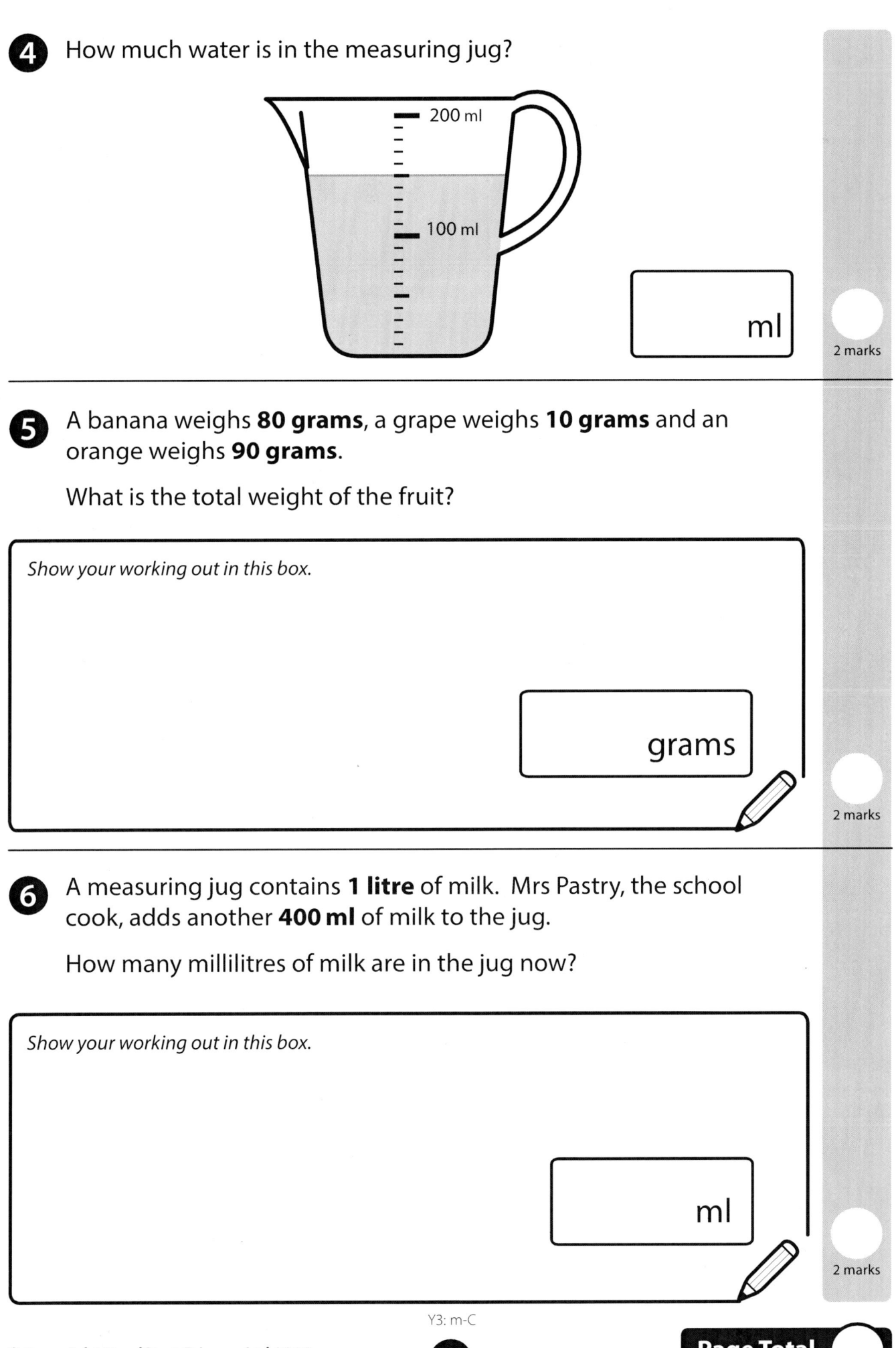

200 ml

100 ml

ml

2 marks

---

5 A banana weighs **80 grams**, a grape weighs **10 grams** and an orange weighs **90 grams**.

What is the total weight of the fruit?

Show your working out in this box.

grams

2 marks

---

6 A measuring jug contains **1 litre** of milk. Mrs Pastry, the school cook, adds another **400 ml** of milk to the jug.

How many millilitres of milk are in the jug now?

Show your working out in this box.

ml

2 marks

Y3: m-C

Page Total

7 Use your ruler to measure the **perimeter** of the rectangle below.

The perimeter measures [ ] cm

---

8 In a sweet shop, fudge costs **£1.75** and licorice costs **£2.00**.

If Liam buys fudge and licorice, how much change will he get from **£5.00**?

Show your working out in this box.

£ [ ]

---

9 Luke has **six £1** coins, **four 20p** coins and **one 10p** coin.

How much does he have altogether?

Show your working out in this box.

£ [ ]

Y3: m-C

Page Total ( )

10 What time is it?

Write your answers in the boxes below the clocks.

a
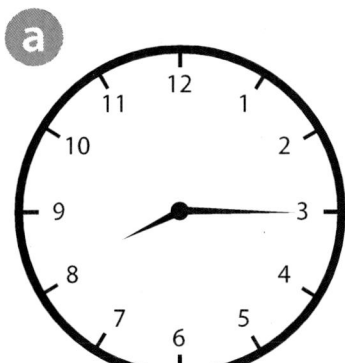

b
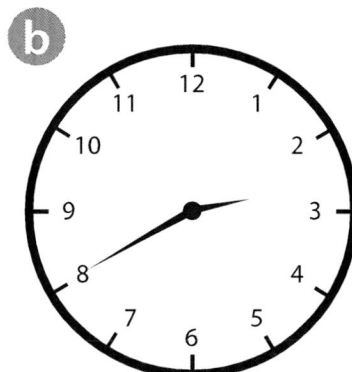

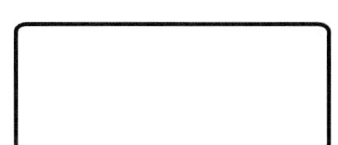

c
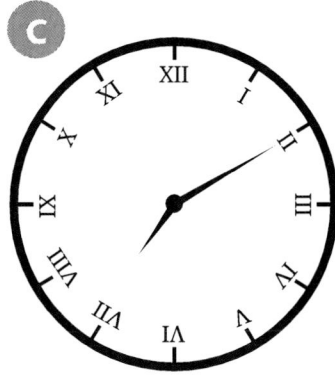

2 marks

11 Draw the times shown on the clocks below.

a
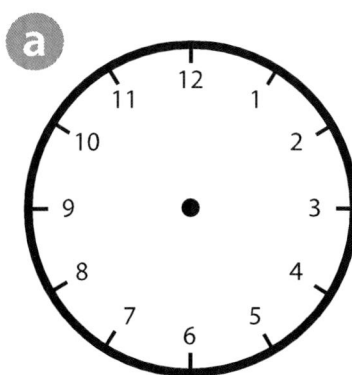

six o'clock

b
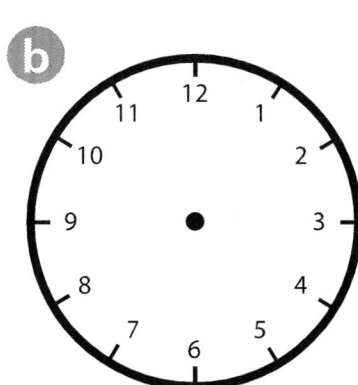

9:25 am

c
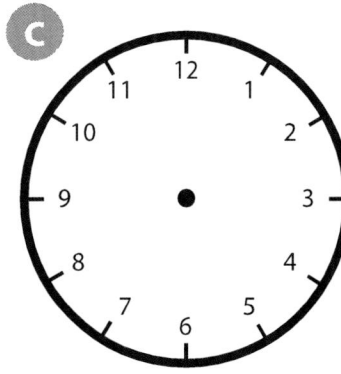

14:00

2 marks

Y3: m-C

Page Total

12 Asif started swimming at the time shown on clock **A.**

He stopped at the time shown on clock **B.**

Estimate how many minutes he swam for.

A

B

minutes

2 marks

---

13 Write **TRUE (T)** or **FALSE (F)** after these statements.

a When it's afternoon, it's **pm**.

b When it's morning, it's **am**.

c It is 24 hours from noon to midnight.

2 marks

Y3: m-C

Page Total

14 Find the matching pairs below. Join them with a line. One has been done for you.

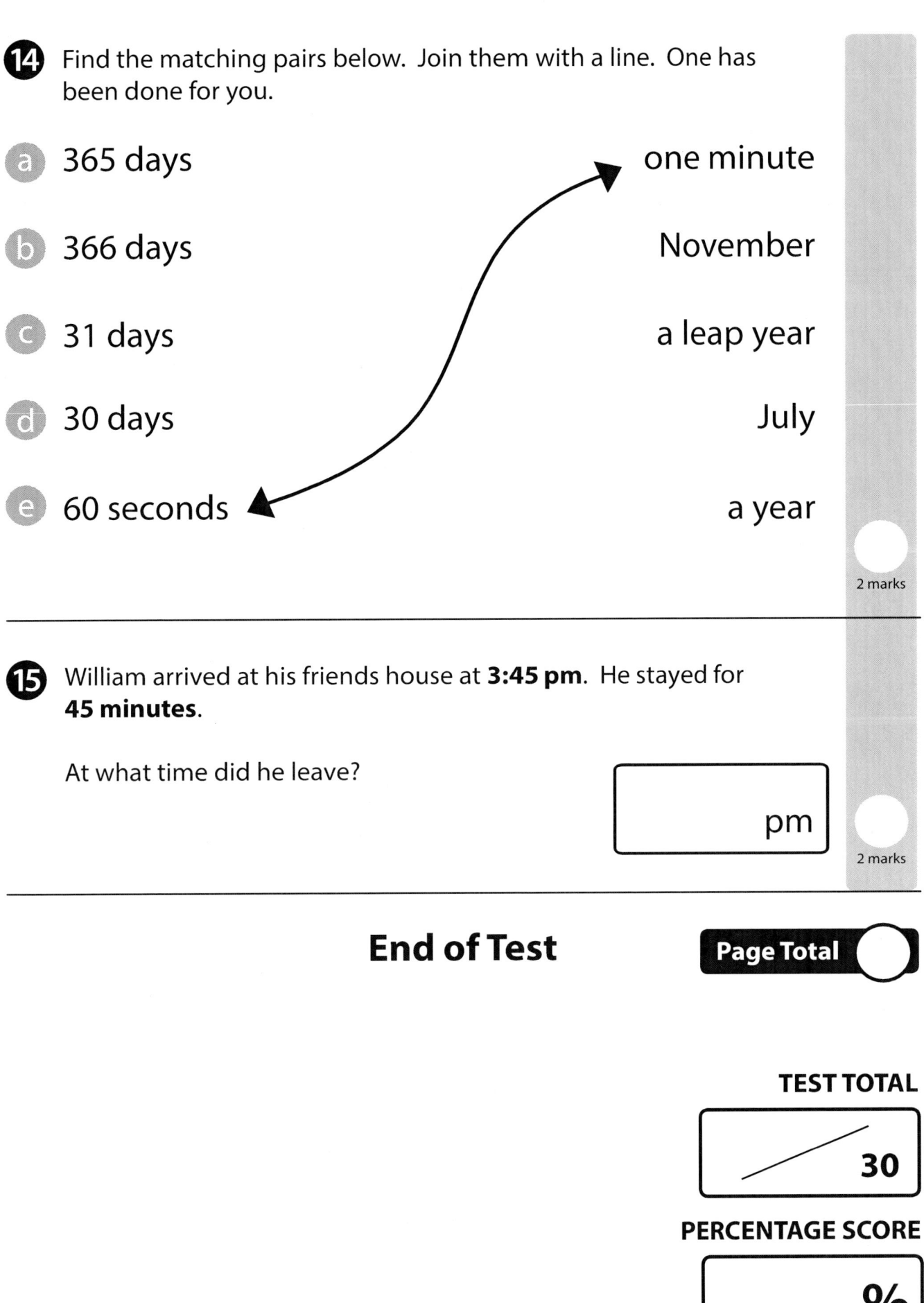

(a) 365 days

(b) 366 days

(c) 31 days

(d) 30 days

(e) 60 seconds

one minute

November

a leap year

July

a year

2 marks

15 William arrived at his friends house at **3:45 pm**. He stayed for **45 minutes**.

At what time did he leave?

pm

2 marks

End of Test

Page Total

TEST TOTAL

30

PERCENTAGE SCORE

%

Y3: m-C

Mathematics Assessment: GEOMETRY - Properties of shapes

Name... Class........................ Date........................

1 Use your ruler to draw a rectangle in the space below.

2 marks

2 Eleanor drew a line **8.5 cm** long as one side of her rectangle. She then decided to round the length of the line up to the next whole number.

How long was Eleanor's line after rounding?

[ ] cm

2 marks

3 Match the 3D shapes to their names. One has been done for you.

a pyramid   **b** cube   **c** cylinder   **d** sphere

2 marks

Y3: g-C

1

Page Total ◯

4 Match the 2D or 3D shapes to their description. One has been done for you.

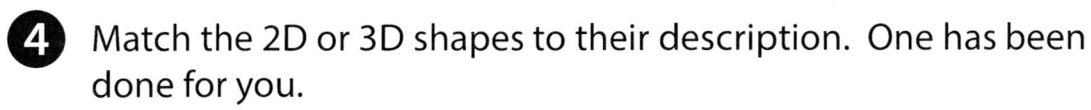

a octagon

> a 3D shape with **1** square face and **4** triangular faces

b rectangle

> a 2D shape with **3** sides and **3** angles

c triangle

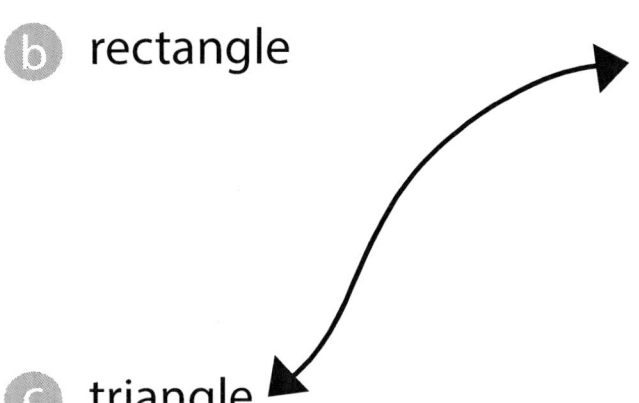

> a 2D shape with **8** sides, **8** angles and **8** lines of symmetry

d square-based pyramid

> a 3D shape with **6** square faces

e cube

> a 2D shape with 4 sides and 4 angles

2 marks

Y3: g-C

Page Total

5 Choose **one** word from the brackets to complete the sentence below.

Many shapes contain a number of _____ .

(colours, angles, patterns)

6 Choose **one** word from the brackets to complete the sentence below.

Amount of _____ is shown by an angle.

(metre, turn, spin)

7 Matthew is facing east. He makes a full turn and ends up facing east again.

How many **right angles** has he turned through?

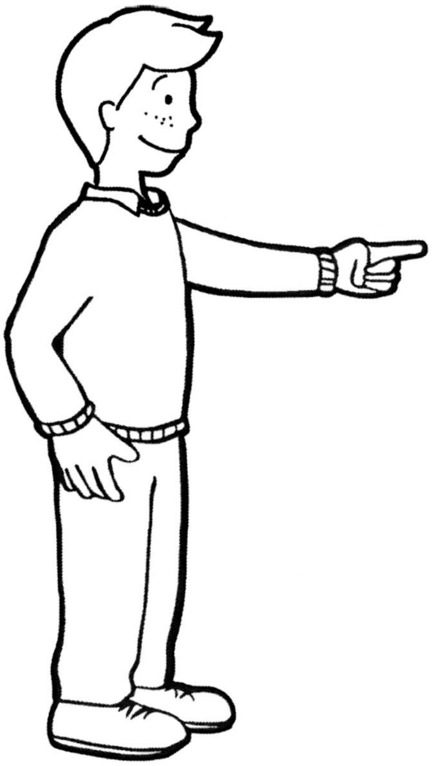

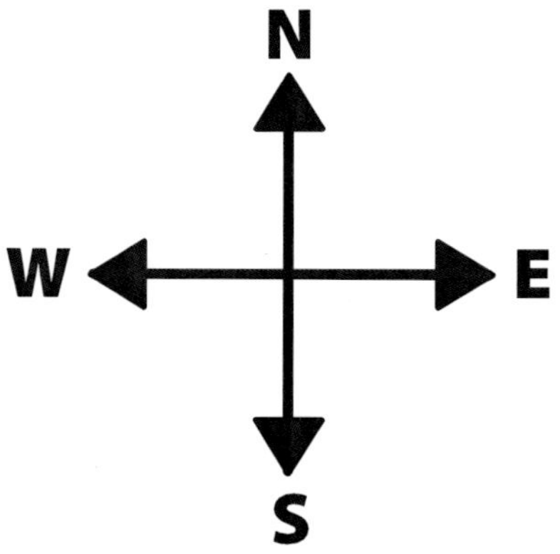

N

W ←——→ **E**

S

right angles

8 Look at the shape below. Put a tick (✔) next to the right angle.

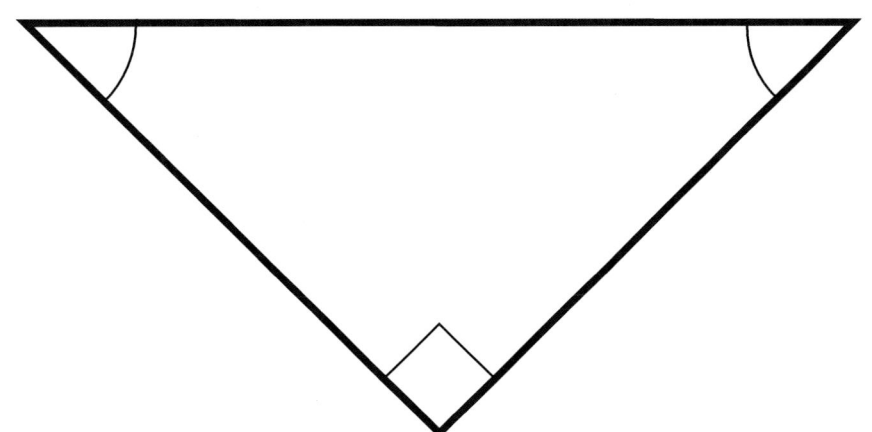

9 Write **TRUE (T)** or **FALSE (F)** after these statements.

a One right angle makes a half-turn.

b One right angle makes a quarter-turn.

c Two right angles make a half-turn.

d Two right angles make a complete turn.

Y3: g-C

Page Total

10 Are the angles below greater than or less than a right angle?

Write '**greater**' or '**less**' in the boxes.

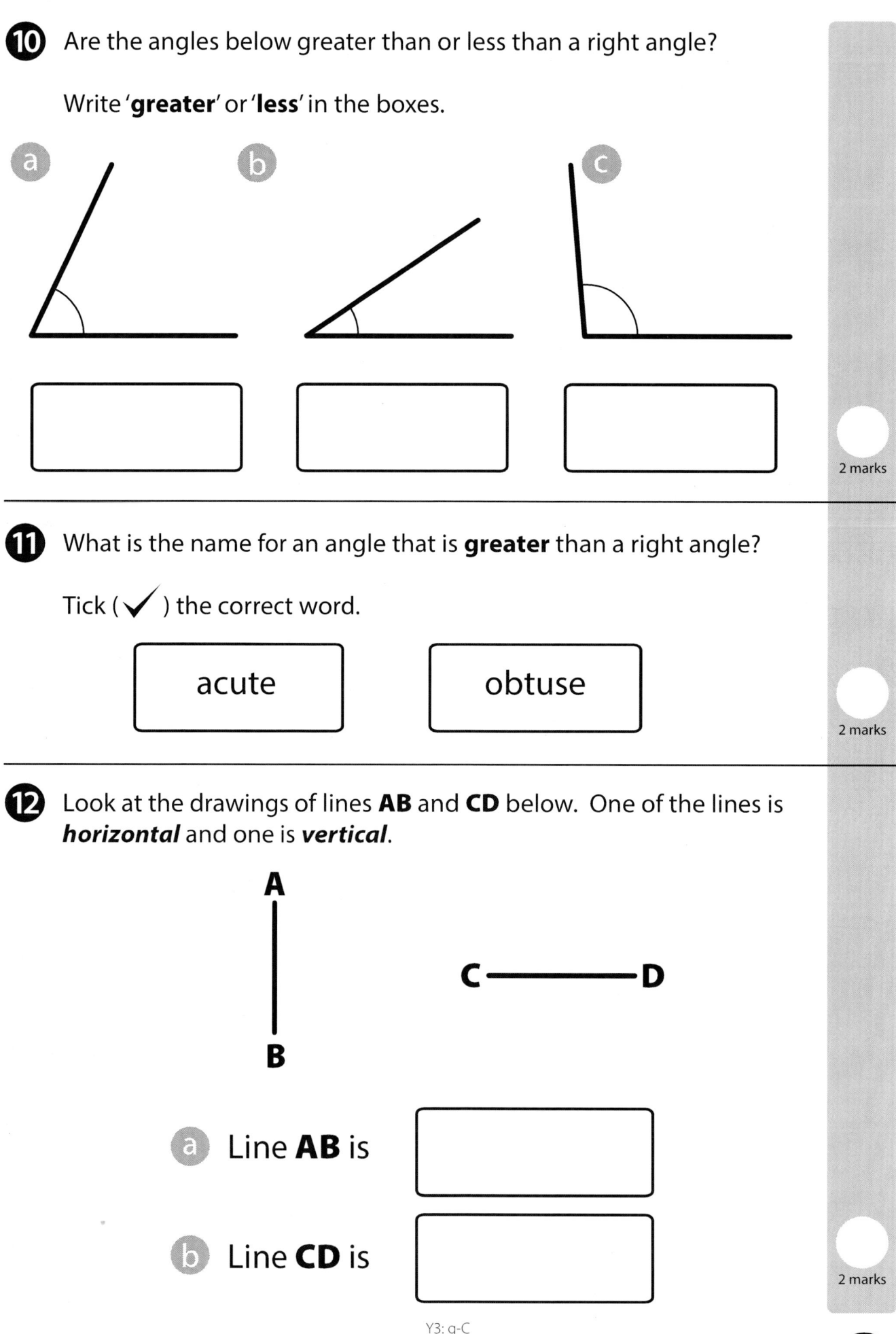

a

b

c

2 marks

11 What is the name for an angle that is **greater** than a right angle?

Tick (✔) the correct word.

acute	obtuse

2 marks

12 Look at the drawings of lines **AB** and **CD** below. One of the lines is *horizontal* and one is *vertical*.

A

B

C——D

a Line **AB** is

b Line **CD** is

2 marks

Y3: g-C

Page Total

13 In the space below, use your ruler to draw a line that is *perpendicular* to line **AB**.

A ———————————————————————— B

2 marks

14 In the space below, use your ruler to draw a line that is *parallel* to line **AB**.

A ———————————————————————— B

2 marks

Y3: g-C

Page Total

15 Write **TRUE (T)** or **FALSE (F)** after these statements.

a) Perpendicular lines are never at right angles to each other.

b) Two parallel lines will never meet.

c) A horizontal line goes from left to right.

d) A vertical line goes straight up and down.

2 marks

End of Test

Page Total

TEST TOTAL

/30

PERCENTAGE SCORE

%

Y3: g-C

Mathematics Assessment: STATISTICS

Name .... Class .... Date ....

Look at the bar chart below.

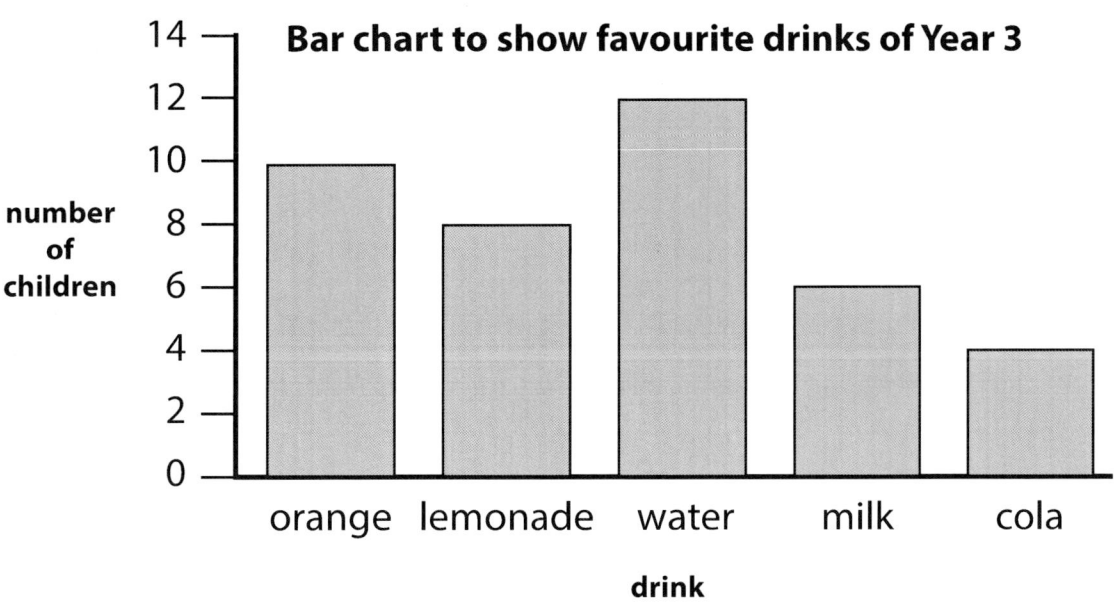

Bar chart to show favourite drinks of Year 3

number of children

Now answer these questions.

1 What is the most popular drink in Year 3?

2 marks

2 How many more people like orange than milk?

people

2 marks

3 If **3** people changed their mind and said they liked lemonade and not orange, how many more people would like lemonade than orange?

people

2 marks

Page Total

Look at the tally chart below.

Animals in the pet shop

Animal		Tally
mouse		 ‖‖‖ ‖‖‖ ‖
bird		 ‖‖‖ ‖
snake		 ‖‖‖
fish		 ‖‖‖ ‖‖‖ ‖‖‖

Now answer these questions.

4 How many birds are in the pet shop?

birds

5 How many more fish are there than mice?

6 Owen says, "There are more mice than there are birds and snakes put together".

Is that true? (Yes or No)

Use this box to explain how you know.

Y3: s-C

Page Total

Look at the pictogram below.

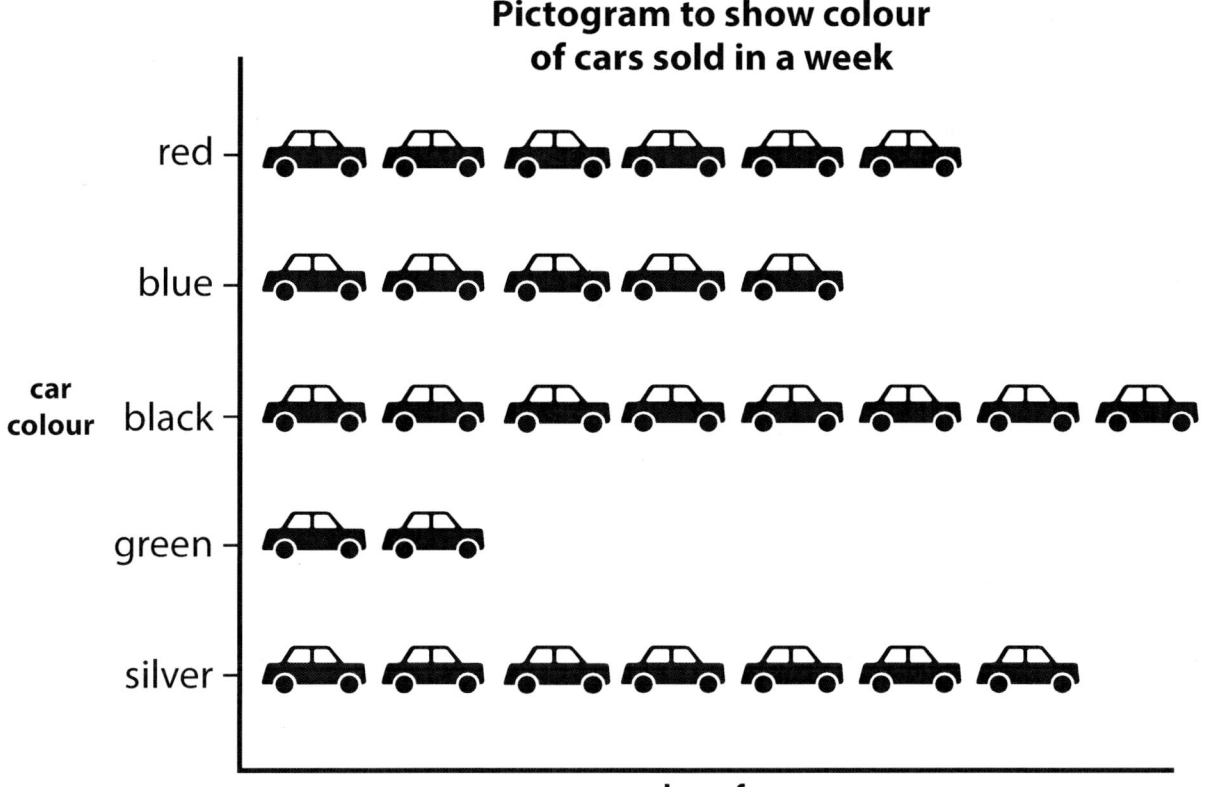

Pictogram to show colour of cars sold in a week

car colour	
red	🚗🚗🚗🚗🚗🚗
blue	🚗🚗🚗🚗🚗
black	🚗🚗🚗🚗🚗🚗🚗🚗
green	🚗🚗
silver	🚗🚗🚗🚗🚗🚗🚗

number of cars

Now answer these questions.

7 How many red and black cars are sold altogether?

8 How many more silver cars are sold than green cars?

9 During the next week, red, black and silver cars sold the same amount as shown on the pictogram. Blue sold **3** more and green sold **2** more.

Draw more cars on the pictogram to show this information.

Y3: s-C

Page Total

Look at the frequency table below.

Day	Number of people swimming
Monday	8
Tuesday	7
Wednesday	4
Thursday	18
Friday	13

Now answer these questions.

10 How many people were swimming on Friday?

people

2 marks

11 How many more people were swimming on Thursday than on Wednesday?

people

2 marks

12 Using the information in the table, write a question that you could ask about the number of people swimming.

Write your question in this box.

2 marks

 **Page Total**

13 Look at the bar chart below.

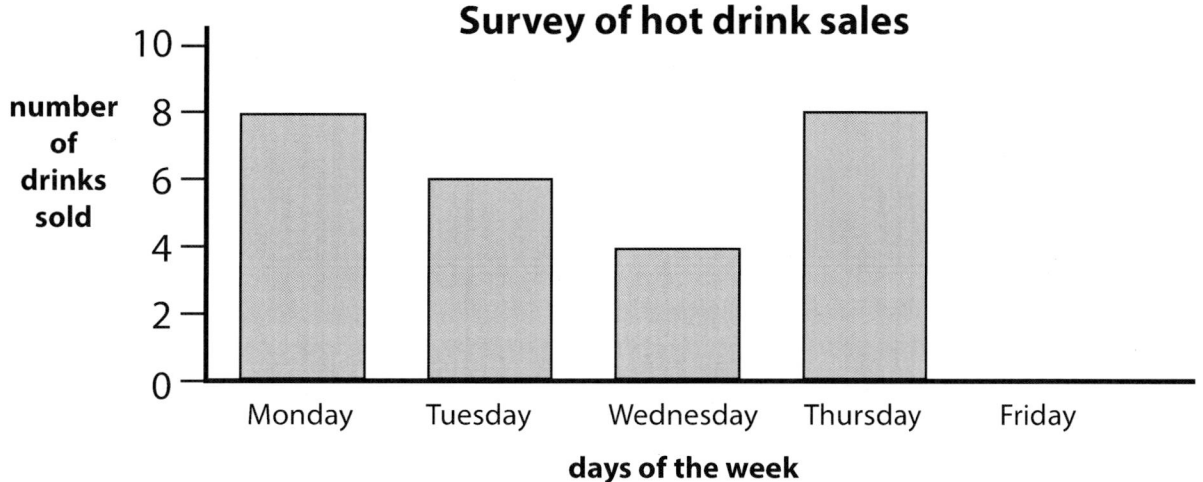

Survey of hot drink sales

number of drinks sold

(a) Firstly, draw in a bar to show that **6** hot drinks were sold on Friday.

(b) Now work out how many hot drinks were sold all week.

Use this box for your working out.

hot drinks

14 During the week after this survey, the weather was much colder.

How do you think the bar chart would be different at the end of the colder week?

Use this box to explain your answer.

Y3: s-C

Page Total

Your class are carrying out a survey to find the children's favourite food. The choice is between:

fruit   pizza   pasta   vegetables

15 Which of the following would be the best way to present the information from the favourite food survey?

Circle your answer.

Carroll diagram   line graph

tally chart   Venn diagram

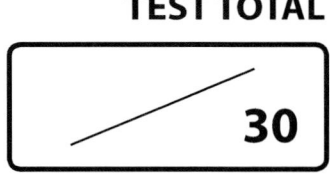

2 marks

End of Test

Page Total ⬤

TEST TOTAL

/ 30

PERCENTAGE SCORE

%

ANSWERS

NUMBER - Number and place value

1) a)8, 20 b)100, 250 c)16, 40
(2 marks for all 3 correct, 1 mark for 2 correct)

2) 117
(2 marks for a correct answer)

3) 674
(2 marks for a correct answer)

4) a)38 b)36 c)694 d)749 e)658 f)25
(2 marks for all 6 correct, 1 mark for 3, 4 or 5 correct)

5) a)400 b)3 c)70
(2 marks for all 3 correct, 1 mark for 2 correct)

6) a)23, 32, 96 b)196, 264, 482 c)189, 819, 918
(2 marks for all 3 correct, 1 mark for 2 correct)

7) a)7 b)40 c)150
(2 marks for all 3 correct, 1 mark for 2 correct)

8) a)answer given b)three – 3 c)fifty six – 56 d)sixty five – 65
e)five hundred and twenty two – 522
f)twenty four – 24
(2 marks for all 5 correct, 1 mark for 3 or 4 correct)

9) a)sixty four b)one hundred and ninety seven c)eight hundred and sixty four d)six hundred and eight
(2 marks for all 4 correct, 1 mark for 2 or 3 correct)

10) a)7 b)2 c)6
(2 marks for all 3 correct, 1 mark for 2 correct)

11) 260 grams
(2 marks for a correct answer)
(1 mark for appropriate working but an incorrect answer)

12) a)972 b)indication of the pattern increasing in steps of 200
(2 marks for 2 correct, 1 mark for 1 correct)

13) 380
(2 marks for a correct answer)
(1 mark for appropriate working but an incorrect answer)

14) £248
(2 marks for a correct answer)
(1 mark for appropriate working but an incorrect answer)

15) 64
(2 marks for a correct answer)

NUMBER - Addition and subtraction

1) a)59 b)53 c)97 d)52 e)71 f)86
(2 marks for all 6 correct, 1 mark for 3, 4 or 5 correct)

2) a)57 b)51 c)94 d)166
(2 marks for all 4 correct, 1 mark for 2 or 3 correct)

3) a)279 b)850 c)647 d)892 e)689 f)359
(2 marks for all 6 correct, 1 mark for 3, 4 or 5 correct)

4) a)384 b)872 c)692 d)673 e)218 f)904
(2 marks for all 6 correct, 1 mark for 3, 4 or 5 correct)

5) a)598 b)932 c)1056 d)743 e)386 f)163
(2 marks for all 6 correct, 1 mark for 3, 4 or 5 correct)

6) a)291 b)814
(2 marks for 2 correct, 1 mark for 1 correct)

7) a)56 b)274
(2 marks for 2 correct, 1 mark for 1 correct)

8) a)514 b)698
(2 marks for 2 correct, 1 mark for 1 correct)

9) 20 + 90 circled
(2 marks for a correct answer)

10) 832, 347
(2 marks for a correct answer)

11) boxes completed appropriately
(2 marks for 3 correct, 1 mark for 2 correct)

12) indication of adding 1
(2 marks for a correct answer)

13) 40 + 600 = 640
(2 marks for all boxes completed correctly)
(1 mark for value boxes completed correctly but an incorrect answer)

14) 16cm
(2 marks for a correct answer) (1 mark for appropriate working but an incorrect answer)

15) 600ml
(2 marks for a correct answer) (1 mark for appropriate working but an incorrect answer)

ANSWERS

NUMBER - Multiplication and division

1) a)6 b)36 c)18 d)8 e)1 f)7
(2 marks for all 6 correct, 1 mark for 3, 4 or 5 correct)

2) a)20 b)36 c)28 d)12 e)2 f)8
(2 marks for all 6 correct, 1 mark for 3, 4 or 5 correct)

3) a)56 b)96 c)40 d)8 e)9 f)11
(2 marks for all 6 correct, 1 mark for 3, 4 or 5 correct)

4) a)48 b)indication of doubling 24
(2 marks for 2 correct, 1 mark for 1 correct)

5) a)69 b)128 c)408 d)23 e)21 f)12
(2 marks for all 6 correct, 1 mark for 3, 4 or 5 correct)

6) a)96 b)3
(2 marks for 2 correct, 1 mark for 1 correct)

7) 20
(2 marks for a correct answer)

8) 8 ÷ 2 = 4 circled
(2 marks for a correct answer)

9) a)78 b)344
(2 marks for 2 correct, 1 mark for 1 correct)

10) a)21 b)121
(2 marks for 2 correct, 1 mark for 1 correct)

11) 272cm
(2 marks for a correct answer) (1 mark for an appropriate written method but an incorrect answer)

12) 24 biscuits
(2 marks for a correct answer) (1 mark for an appropriate written method but an incorrect answer)

13) 304cm
(2 marks for a correct answer) (1 mark for appropriate working but an incorrect answer)

14) 12 Mr Potato Heads
(2 marks for a correct answer) (1 mark for appropriate working but an incorrect answer)

15) 112 rides
(2 marks for a correct answer) (1 mark for appropriate working but an incorrect answer)

NUMBER - Fractions

1) a)4/10 b)6/10
(2 marks for 2 correct, 1 mark for 1 correct)

2) a)3 tenths b)shading shows 6 tenths in total
(2 marks for 2 correct, 1 mark for 1 correct)

3) a)answer given
b)0.1 = 1/10 c)0.3 = 3/10
d)0.8 = 8/10
(2 marks for 3 correct, 1 mark for 2 correct)

4) a)0.6 b)0.7 c)0.9
(2 marks for 3 correct, 1 mark for 2 correct)

5) 2/5 circled
(2 marks for a correct answer)

6) arrow drawn in correct place on the number line
(2 marks for a correct answer)

7) 1/4
(2 marks for a correct answer)

8) 1/2 of 16 litres ticked
(2 marks for a correct answer)

9) a)5 b)7
(2 marks for 2 correct, 1 mark for 1 correct)

10) a)1/2 = 2/4 b)1/3 = 2/6
c)answer given
d)1/5 = 2/10
(2 marks for all 3 correct, 1 mark for 2 correct)

11) 4 bars shaded on shape B
(2 marks for a correct answer)

12) a)4/5 b)5/7
(2 marks for 2 correct, 1 mark for 1 correct)

13) a)3/8 b)3/6
(2 marks for 2 correct, 1 mark for 1 correct)

14) a)2/6, 3/6, 4/6, 5/6 b)1/12, 1/9, 1/4, 1/2
(2 marks for 2 correct, 1 mark for 1 correct)

15) 3/5
(2 marks for a correct answer) (1 mark for appropriate working but an incorrect answer)

ANSWERS

MEASUREMENT

1) 2cm 3mm
(2 marks for a correct answer)

2) 3kg
(2 marks for a correct answer)

3) Nik (143cm tall)
(2 marks for a correct answer)

4) 150ml
(2 marks for a correct answer)

5) 190 grams
(2 marks for a correct answer) (1 mark for appropriate working but an incorrect answer)

6) 1200ml
(2 marks for a correct answer) (1 mark for appropriate working but an incorrect answer)

7) 24cm
(2 marks for a correct answer)

8) £1.25
(2 marks for a correct answer) (1 mark for appropriate working but an incorrect answer)

9) £5.80
(2 marks for a correct answer) (1 mark for appropriate working but an incorrect answer)

10) a)3:30 b)8:25 c)7:55
(or alternative ways of writing the time)
(2 marks for all 3 correct, 1 mark for 2 correct)

11) a)four o'clock drawn with appropriate accuracy
b)11:30am drawn with appropriate accuracy
c)18:00 drawn with appropriate accuracy
(2 marks for all 3 correct, 1 mark for 2 correct)

12) 8 or 9 minutes
(2 marks for a correct answer) (1 mark for 7 minutes)

13) a)F b)T c)F
(2 marks for all 3 correct, 1 mark for 2 correct)

14) a)60 seconds matched to one minute
b)answer given
c)31 days matched to May
d)366 days matched to a leap year
e)365 days matched to a year
(2 marks for all 4 correct, 1 mark for 2 or 3 correct)

15) 5:00pm
(2 marks for a correct answer)

GEOMETRY - Properties of shapes

1) rectangle appropriately drawn
(2 marks for a correct answer)

2) 10cm
(2 marks for a correct answer)

3) a)pyramid matched to 3rd shape
c)cylinder matched to 2nd shape
d)cuboid matched to 1st shape
(2 marks for all 3 correct, 1 mark for 2 correct)

4) a)hexagon matched to a 2D shape with 6 sides, 6 angles and 6 lines of symmetry
b)sphere matched to a 3D shape that is round like a football
c)triangle matched to a 2D shape with 3 sides and 3 angles
d)prism matched to a 3D shape with 2 triangular faces and 3 rectangular faces
e)answer given
(2 marks for all 4 correct, 1 mark for 2 or 3 correct)

5) property
(2 marks for a correct answer)

6) turn
(2 marks for a correct answer)

7) 2 right angles
(2 marks for a correct answer)

8) right angle ticked appropriately
(2 marks for a correct answer)

9) a)F b)T c)T d)F
(2 marks for all 4 correct, 1 mark for 2 or 3 correct)

10) a)less b)greater c)less
(2 marks for all 3 correct, 1 mark for 2 correct)

11) obtuse ticked
(2 marks for a correct answer)

12) a)vertical b)horizontal
(2 marks for 2 correct, 1 mark for 1 correct)

13) perpendicular line drawn appropriately
(2 marks for a correct answer)

14) parallel line drawn appropriately
(2 marks for a correct answer)

15) a)T b)T c)F d)F
(2 marks for all 4 correct, 1 mark for 2 or 3 correct)

ANSWERS

STATISTICS

1) netball
(2 marks for a correct answer)

2) 8 people
(2 marks for a correct answer)

3) 2 people
(2 marks for a correct answer)

4) 3 cows
(2 marks for a correct answer)

5) 4
(2 marks for a correct answer)

6) yes; indication of 9 (pigs) being greater than 3 (cows) + 5 (sheep) = 8
(2 marks for a correct answer)

7) 9
(2 marks for a correct answer)

8) 4
(2 marks for a correct answer)

9) bikes drawn appropriately on pictogram
(2 marks for a correct answer)

10) 12 cars
(2 marks for a correct answer)

11) 11 cars
(2 marks for a correct answer)

12) appropriate question written
(2 marks for a correct answer)

13) a)Tuesday bar drawn to 8 with appropriate accuracy
b)30 cold drinks
(2 marks for 2 correct, 1 mark for 1 correct)

14) indication that more cold drinks would be sold due to hotter weather
(2 marks for a correct answer)

15) tally chart circled
(2 marks for a correct answer)

ANSWERS

NUMBER - Number and place value

1) a)4, 20 b)150, 250 c)24, 32
*(2 marks for all 3 correct, 1 mark
for 2 correct)*

2) 126
(2 marks for a correct answer)

3) 564
(2 marks for a correct answer)

4) a)44 b)47 c)442 d)486 e)729 f)76
*(2 marks for all 6 correct, 1 mark for 3,
4 or 5 correct)*

5) a)500 b)9 c)40
*(2 marks for all 3 correct, 1 mark
for 2 correct)*

6) a)17, 26, 84 b)167, 358, 528 c)178,
718, 817
*(2 marks for all 3 correct, 1 mark
for 2 correct)*

7) a)8 b)40 c)250
*(2 marks for all 3 correct, 1 mark
for 2 correct)*

8) a)fourteen – 14 b)answer given
c)forty nine - 49 d)seventy four – 74
e)four hundred and thirty two – 432
f)twenty eight – 28
*(2 marks for all 5 correct, 1 mark for
3 or 4 correct)*

9) a)fifty six b)one hundred and
eighty six
c)seven hundred and fifty eight
d)three hundred and four
*(2 marks for all 4 correct, 1 mark for
2 or 3 correct)*

10) a)9 b)2 c)8
*(2 marks for all 3 correct, 1 mark
for 2 correct)*

11) 380 grams
(2 marks for a correct answer)
*(1 mark for appropriate working but an
incorrect answer)*

12) a)894
b)indication of the pattern increasing
in steps of 200
(2 marks for 2 correct, 1 mark for 1 correct)

13) 460
(2 marks for a correct answer)
*(1 mark for appropriate working but
an incorrect answer)*

14) £464
(2 marks for a correct answer)
*(1 mark for appropriate working but
an incorrect answer)*

15) 56
(2 marks for a correct answer)

NUMBER - Addition and subtraction

1) a)49 b)73 c)84 d)33 e)61 f)78
*(2 marks for all 6 correct, 1 mark for 3,
4 or 5 correct)*

2) a)59 b)51 c)83 d)172
*(2 marks for all 4 correct, 1 mark for
2 or 3 correct)*

3) a)366 b)740 c)557 d)781
e)869 f)469
*(2 marks for all 6 correct, 1 mark for 3,
4 or 5 correct)*

4) a)265 b)766 c)598 d)556
e)336 f)807
*(2 marks for all 6 correct, 1 mark for 3,
4 or 5 correct)*

5) a)567 b)885 c)1046 d)565
e)595 f)376
*(2 marks for all 6 correct, 1 mark for 3,
4 or 5 correct)*

6) a)371 b)821
(2 marks for 2 correct, 1 mark for 1 correct)

7) a)37 b)277
(2 marks for 2 correct, 1 mark for 1 correct)

8) a)618 b)769
(2 marks for 2 correct, 1 mark for 1 correct)

9) 40 + 80 circled
(2 marks for a correct answer)

10) 834, 438
(2 marks for a correct answer)

11) boxes completed appropriately
(2 marks for 3 correct, 1 mark for 2 correct)

12) indication of adding 1
(2 marks for a correct answer)

13) 60 + 700 = 760
(2 marks for all boxes completed correctly)
*(1 mark for value boxes completed
correctly but an incorrect answer)*

14) 39cm
(2 marks for a correct answer)
*(1 mark for appropriate working but an
incorrect answer)*

15) 400ml
(2 marks for a correct answer)
*(1 mark for appropriate working but an
incorrect answer)*

ANSWERS

NUMBER - Multiplication and division

1) a)9 b)24 c)27 d)12 e)2 f)10
(2 marks for all 6 correct, 1 mark for 3, 4 or 5 correct)

2) a)24 b)32 c)48 d)11 e)3 f)9
(2 marks for all 6 correct, 1 mark for 3, 4 or 5 correct)

3) a)64 b)48 c)88 d)12 e)5 f)10
(2 marks for all 6 correct, 1 mark for 3, 4 or 5 correct)

4) a)64
b)indication of doubling 32
(2 marks for 2 correct, 1 mark for 1 correct)

5) a)99 b)168 c)568 d)32 e)12 f)12
(2 marks for all 6 correct, 1 mark for 3, 4 or 5 correct)

6) a)96 b)4
(2 marks for 2 correct, 1 mark for 1 correct)

7) 25
(2 marks for a correct answer)

8) 9 ÷ 3 = 3 circled
(2 marks for a correct answer)

9) a)112 b)608
(2 marks for 2 correct, 1 mark for 1 correct)

10) a)32 b)231
(2 marks for 2 correct, 1 mark for 1 correct)

11) 201cm
(2 marks for a correct answer)
(1 mark for an appropriate written method but an incorrect answer)

12) 26 chocolates
(2 marks for a correct answer)
(1 mark for an appropriate written method but an incorrect answer)

13) 261cm
(2 marks for a correct answer)
(1 mark for appropriate working but an incorrect answer)

14) 28 outfits
(2 marks for a correct answer)
(1 mark for appropriate working but an incorrect answer)

15) 142 taxis
(2 marks for a correct answer)
(1 mark for appropriate working but an incorrect answer)

NUMBER - Fractions

1) a)8/10 b)5/10
(2 marks for 2 correct, 1 mark for 1 correct)

2) a)5 tenths b)shading shows 7 tenths in total
(2 marks for 2 correct, 1 mark for 1 correct)

3) a)0.4 = 4/10 b)0.9 = 9/10 c)0.2 = 2/10 d)answer given
(2 marks for 3 correct, 1 mark for 2 correct)

4) a)0.4 b)0.8 c)0.2
(2 marks for 3 correct, 1 mark for 2 correct)

5) 3/5 circled
(2 marks for a correct answer)

6) arrow drawn in correct place on the number line
(2 marks for a correct answer)

7) 3/4
(2 marks for a correct answer)

8) 1/2 of 12 litres ticked
(2 marks for a correct answer)

9) a)6 b)9
(2 marks for 2 correct, 1 mark for 1 correct)

10) a)1/2 = 2/4 b)answer given c)1/4 = 2/8 d)1/5 = 2/10
(2 marks for all 3 correct, 1 mark for 2 correct)

11) 2 bars shaded on shape B
(2 marks for a correct answer)

12) a)3/4 b)6/9
(2 marks for 2 correct, 1 mark for 1 correct)

13) a)2/5 b)2/8
(2 marks for 2 correct, 1 mark for 1 correct)

14) a)1/7, 3/7, 5/7, 6/7 b)1/10, 1/8, 1/5, 1/3
(2 marks for 2 correct, 1 mark for 1 correct)

15) 5/7
(2 marks for a correct answer) (1 mark for appropriate working but an incorrect answer)

ANSWERS

MEASUREMENT

1) 1cm 6mm
(2 marks for a correct answer)

2) 7kg
(2 marks for a correct answer)

3) Max (138cm tall)
(2 marks for a correct answer)

4) 50ml
(2 marks for a correct answer)

5) 190 grams
(2 marks for a correct answer) (1 mark for appropriate working but an incorrect answer)

6) 1300ml
(2 marks for a correct answer) (1 mark for appropriate working but an incorrect answer)

7) 28cm
(2 marks for a correct answer)

8) £2.45
(2 marks for a correct answer) (1 mark for appropriate working but an incorrect answer)

9) £7.90
(2 marks for a correct answer) (1 mark for appropriate working but an incorrect answer)

10) a)4:45 b)10:20 c)5:50
(or alternative ways of writing the time)
(2 marks for all 3 correct, 1 mark for 2 correct)

11) a)two o'clock drawn with appropriate accuracy
b)6:15am drawn with appropriate accuracy
c)19:00 drawn with appropriate accuracy
(2 marks for all 3 correct, 1 mark for 2 correct)

12) 11 or 12 minutes
(2 marks for a correct answer) (1 mark for 13 minutes)

13) a)T b)F c)T
(2 marks for all 3 correct, 1 mark for 2 correct)

14) a)366 days matched to a leap year
b)30 days matched to April
c)365 days matched to a year
d)60 seconds matched to one minute
e)answer given
(2 marks for all 4 correct, 1 mark for 2 or 3 correct)

15) 7:15pm
(2 marks for a correct answer)

GEOMETRY - Properties of shapes

1) rectangle appropriately drawn
(2 marks for a correct answer)

2) 8cm
(2 marks for a correct answer)

3) a)prism matched to 3rd shape
b)cube matched to 4th shape
d)cuboid matched to 1st shape
(2 marks for all 3 correct, 1 mark for 2 correct)

4) a)pentagon matched to a 2D shape with 5 sides, 5 angles and 5 lines of symmetry
b)prism matched to a 3D shape with 2 triangular faces and 3 rectangular faces
c)circle matched to a 2D shape with 1 curved side and no angles
d)answer given
e)square matched to a 2D shape with 4 equal sides and 4 equal angles
(2 marks for all 4 correct, 1 mark for 2 or 3 correct)

5) angles
(2 marks for a correct answer)

6) Angles
(2 marks for a correct answer)

7) 2 right angles
(2 marks for a correct answer)

8) right angle ticked appropriately
(2 marks for a correct answer)

9) a)F b)T c)T d)T
(2 marks for all 4 correct, 1 mark for 2 or 3 correct)

10) a)less b)greater c)greater
(2 marks for all 3 correct, 1 mark for 2 correct)

11) acute ticked
(2 marks for a correct answer)

12) a)horizontal b)vertical
(2 marks for 2 correct, 1 mark for 1 correct)

13) perpendicular line drawn appropriately
(2 marks for a correct answer)

14) parallel line drawn appropriately
(2 marks for a correct answer)

15) a)F b)T c)F d)T
(2 marks for all 4 correct, 1 mark for 2 or 3 correct)

ANSWERS

STATISTICS

1) orange
(2 marks for a correct answer)

2) 6 people
(2 marks for a correct answer)

3) 4 people
(2 marks for a correct answer)

4) 5 bears
(2 marks for a correct answer)

5) 8
(2 marks for a correct answer)

6) no; indication of 12 (penguins) being less than 4 (tigers) + 9 (camels) = 13
(2 marks for a correct answer)

7) 15
(2 marks for a correct answer)

8) 4
(2 marks for a correct answer)

9) t-shirts drawn appropriately on pictogram
(2 marks for a correct answer)

10) 11 children
(2 marks for a correct answer)

11) 8 children
(2 marks for a correct answer)

12) appropriate question written
(2 marks for a correct answer)

13) a)Thursday bar drawn to 8 with appropriate accuracy
b)28 ice creams
(2 marks for 2 correct, 1 mark for 1 correct)

14) indication that fewer ice creams would be sold due to colder weather
(2 marks for a correct answer)

15) tally chart circled
(2 marks for a correct answer)

ANSWERS

NUMBER - Number and place value

1) a)8, 12 b)50, 250 c)16, 40
(2 marks for all 3 correct, 1 mark for 2 correct)

2) 104
(2 marks for a correct answer)

3) 436
(2 marks for a correct answer)

4) a)56 b)28 c)575 d)356 e)394 f)87
(2 marks for all 6 correct, 1 mark for 3, 4 or 5 correct)

5) a)700 b)2 c)60
(2 marks for all 3 correct, 1 mark for 2 correct)

6) a)31, 47, 82 b)248, 397, 543
c)156, 516, 615
(2 marks for all 3 correct, 1 mark for 2 correct)

7) a)9 b)40 c)350
(2 marks for all 3 correct, 1 mark for 2 correct)

8) a)eighteen – 18 b)seven - 7
c) answer given d)ninety seven – 97
e)three hundred and sixty four – 364
f)thirty – 30
(2 marks for all 5 correct, 1 mark for 3 or 4 correct)

9) a)eighty six b)one hundred and forty three
c)six hundred and forty nine d)eight hundred and six
(2 marks for all 4 correct, 1 mark for 2 or 3 correct)

10) a)6 b)2 c)5
(2 marks for all 3 correct, 1 mark for 2 correct)

11) 460 grams
(2 marks for a correct answer) (1 mark for appropriate working but an incorrect answer)

12) a)987
b)indication of the pattern increasing in steps of 200
(2 marks for 2 correct, 1 mark for 1 correct)

13) 740
(2 marks for a correct answer)
(1 mark for appropriate working but an incorrect answer)

14) £422
(2 marks for a correct answer)
(1 mark for appropriate working but an incorrect answer)

15) 96
(2 marks for a correct answer)

NUMBER - Addition and subtraction

1) a)36 b)53 c)74 d)43 e)81 f)68
(2 marks for all 6 correct, 1 mark for 3, 4 or 5 correct)

2) a)79 b)42 c)96 d)151
(2 marks for all 4 correct, 1 mark for 2 or 3 correct)

3) a)629 b)360 c)476 d)484
e)939 f)869
(2 marks for all 6 correct, 1 mark for 3, 4 or 5 correct)

4) a)559 b)657 c)798 d)653
e)228 f)404
(2 marks for all 6 correct, 1 mark for 3, 4 or 5 correct)

5) a)626 b)678 c)1024 d)543
e)386 f)363
(2 marks for all 6 correct, 1 mark for 3, 4 or 5 correct)

6) a)465 b)816
(2 marks for 2 correct, 1 mark for 1 correct)

7) a)16 b)267
(2 marks for 2 correct, 1 mark for 1 correct)

8) a)417 b)586
(2 marks for 2 correct, 1 mark for 1 correct)

9) 30 + 70 circled
(2 marks for a correct answer)

10) 661, 297
(2 marks for a correct answer)

11) boxes completed appropriately
(2 marks for 3 correct, 1 mark for 2 correct)

12) indication of adding 1
(2 marks for a correct answer)

13) 70 + 800 = 870
(2 marks for all boxes completed correctly)
(1 mark for value boxes completed correctly but an incorrect answer)

14) 49cm
(2 marks for a correct answer)
(1 mark for appropriate working but an incorrect answer)

15) 400ml
(2 marks for a correct answer)
(1 mark for appropriate working but an incorrect answer)

ANSWERS

NUMBER - Multiplication and division

1) a)12 b)21 c)15 d)11 e)9 f)4
(2 marks for all 6 correct, 1 mark for 3, 4 or 5 correct)

2) a)44 b)12 c)40 d)4 e)6 f)1
(2 marks for all 6 correct, 1 mark for 3, 4 or 5 correct)

3) a)72 b)32 c)96 d)1 e)3 f)7
(2 marks for all 6 correct, 1 mark for 3, 4 or 5 correct)

4) a)32
b) indication of doubling 16
(2 marks for 2 correct, 1 mark for 1 correct)

5) a)96 b)208 c)488 d)13 e)22 f)12
(2 marks for all 6 correct, 1 mark for 3,4 or 5 correct)

6) a)96 b)8
(2 marks for 2 correct, 1 mark for 1 correct)

7) 30
(2 marks for a correct answer)

8) 12 ÷ 4 = 3 circled
(2 marks for a correct answer)

9) a)87 b)520
(2 marks for 2 correct, 1 mark for 1 correct)

10) a)23 b)112
(2 marks for 2 correct, 1 mark for 1 correct)

11) 184cm
(2 marks for a correct answer)
(1 mark for an appropriate written method but an incorrect answer)

12) 121 cars
(2 marks for a correct answer)
(1 mark for an appropriate written method but an incorrect answer)

13) 512cm
(2 marks for a correct answer)
(1 mark for appropriate working but an incorrect answer)

14) 48 outfits
(2 marks for a correct answer)
(1 mark for appropriate working but an incorrect answer)

15) 121 cages
(2 marks for a correct answer)
(1 mark for appropriate working but an incorrect answer)

NUMBER - Fractions

1) a)4/10 b)8/10
(2 marks for 2 correct, 1 mark for 1 correct)

2) a)4 tenths b)shading shows 8 tenths in total
(2 marks for 2 correct, 1 mark for 1 correct)

3) a)0.3 = 3/10 b)0.7 = 7/10 c)0.6 = 6/10 d)answer given
(2 marks for 3 correct, 1 mark for 2 correct)

4) a)0.3 b)0.5 c)0.1
(2 marks for 3 correct, 1 mark for 2 correct)

5) 3/5 circled
(2 marks for a correct answer)

6) arrow drawn in correct place on the number line
(2 marks for a correct answer)

7) 1/4
(2 marks for a correct answer)

8) 1/3 of 27 litres ticked
(2 marks for a correct answer)

9) a)5 b)9
(2 marks for 2 correct, 1 mark for 1 correct)

10) a)1/5 = 2/10 b)answer given c)1/3 = 2/6 d)1/2 = 2/4
(2 marks for all 3 correct, 1 mark for 2 correct)

11) 2 bars shaded on shape B
(2 marks for a correct answer)

12) a)5/6 b)5/8
(2 marks for 2 correct, 1 mark for 1 correct)

13) a)6/9 b)1/7
(2 marks for 2 correct, 1 mark for 1 correct)

14) a)1/8, 3/8, 4/8, 7/8 b)1/11, 1/7, 1/6, 1/2
(2 marks for 2 correct, 1 mark for 1 correct)

15) 6/9
(2 marks for a correct answer)
(1 mark for appropriate working but an incorrect answer)

ANSWERS

MEASUREMENT

1) 2cm 8mm
(2 marks for a correct answer)

2) 9kg
(2 marks for a correct answer)

3)Eva (1m 42cm tall)
(2 marks for a correct answer)

4)150ml
(2 marks for a correct answer)

5) 180 grams
(2 marks for a correct answer) (1 mark for appropriate working but an incorrect answer)

6) 1400ml
(2 marks for a correct answer) (1 mark for appropriate working but an incorrect answer)

7) 26cm
(2 marks for a correct answer)

8) £1.25
(2 marks for a correct answer) (1 mark for appropriate working but an incorrect answer)

9) £6.90
(2 marks for a correct answer) (1 mark for appropriate working but an incorrect answer)

10) a)8:15 b)2:40 c)7:10
(or alternative ways of writing the time)
(2 marks for all 3 correct, 1 mark for 2 correct)

11) a)six o'clock drawn with appropriate accuracy
b)9:25pm drawn with appropriate accuracy
c)14:00 drawn with appropriate accuracy
(2 marks for all 3 correct, 1 mark for 2 correct)

12) 13 or 14 minutes
(2 marks for a correct answer)
(1 mark for 12 minutes)

13) a)T b)T c)F
(2 marks for all 3 correct, 1 mark for 2 correct)

14) a)365 days matched to a year
b)366 days matched to a leap year
c)31 days matched to July
d)30 days matched to November
e)answer given
(2 marks for all 4 correct, 1 mark for 2 or 3 correct)

15) 4:30pm
(2 marks for a correct answer)

GEOMETRY - Properties of shapes

1) rectangle appropriately drawn
(2 marks for a correct answer)

2) 9cm
(2 marks for a correct answer)

3) a)pyramid matched to 3rd shape
b)cube matched to 4th shape
d)sphere matched to 1st shape
(2 marks for all 3 correct, 1 mark for 2 correct)

4) a)octagon matched to a 2D shape with 8 sides, 8 angles and 8 lines of symmetry
b)rectangle matched to a 2D shape with four sides and four angles
c)answer given
d)square-based pyramid matched to a 3D shape with 1 square face and 4 triangular faces
e)cube matched to a 3D shape with 6 square faces
(2 marks for all 4 correct, 1 mark for 2 or 3 correct)

5) angles
(2 marks for a correct answer)

6) turn
(2 marks for a correct answer)

7) 4 right angles
(2 marks for a correct answer)

8) right angle ticked appropriately
(2 marks for a correct answer)

9) a)F b)T c)T d)F
(2 marks for all 4 correct, 1 mark for 2 or 3 correct)

10) a)less b)less c)greater
(2 marks for all 3 correct, 1 mark for 2 correct)

11) obtuse ticked
(2 marks for a correct answer)

12) a)vertical b)horizontal
(2 marks for 2 correct, 1 mark for 1 correct)

13) perpendicular line drawn appropriately
(2 marks for a correct answer)

14) parallel line drawn appropriately
(2 marks for a correct answer)

15) a)F b)T c)T d)T
(2 marks for all 4 correct, 1 mark for 2 or 3 correct)

ANSWERS

STATISTICS

1) water
(2 marks for a correct answer)

2) 4 people
(2 marks for a correct answer)

3) 4 people
(2 marks for a correct answer)

4) 7 birds
(2 marks for a correct answer)

5) 3
(2 marks for a correct answer)

6) yes; indication of 12 (mice) being more than 7 (birds) + 4 (snakes) = 11
(2 marks for a correct answer)

7) 14
(2 marks for a correct answer)

8) 5
(2 marks for a correct answer)

9) cars drawn appropriately on pictogram
(2 marks for a correct answer)

10) 13 people
(2 marks for a correct answer)

11) 14 people
(2 marks for a correct answer)

12) appropriate question written
(2 marks for a correct answer)

13) a)Friday bar drawn to 6 with appropriate accuracy
b)32 hot drinks
(2 marks for 2 correct, 1 mark for 1 correct)

14) indication that more hot drinks would be sold due to colder weather
(2 marks for a correct answer)

15) tally chart circled
(2 marks for a correct answer)

Please mark as
TEST
A B or C

Year 3: NUMBER - Number and place value

Children's Names

| Percentage per question |
| Total correct per question |

Question Objectives

1.	count from zero in multiples of 4, 50 and 8 (npv 1)
2.	count forwards in tens (npv 1)
3.	count backwards in hundreds (npv 1)
4.	find 10 or 100 more or less than a given number (npv 1)
5.	recognise the place value of each digit in a three-digit number – hundreds, tens, ones (npv 2)
6.	compare and order numbers up to 1000 (npv 3)
7.	apply partitioning related to place value (npv 4)
8.	read numbers up to 1000 in numerals and words (npv 5)
9.	write numbers up to 1000 in words (npv 5)
10.	solve a problem involving place value and missing numbers (npv 6)
11.	solve a problem involving counting in multiples of 10 (npv 6)
12.	solve a problem and explain the method involving counting in multiples of 100 (npv 6)
13.	solve a problem involving place value (npv 6)
14.	solve a problem involving counting back in multiples of 10 and 100 (npv 6)
15.	solve a problem involving finding a missing number from clues (npv 6)

Children's Scores

Percentages

Enlarge to A3 for added clarity

Year 3: NUMBER - Addition and subtraction

Please mark as

TEST
A B or C

	Total correct per question	Percentage per question

Children's Names

Question Objectives

1.	add and subtract mentally a two-digit number and a one-digit number (as 1)
2.	add and subtract mentally a two/three-digit number and a two-digit number (as 1)
3.	add and subtract mentally a three-digit number and ones (as 1)
4.	add and subtract mentally a three-digit number and tens (as 1)
5.	add and subtract mentally a three-digit number and hundreds (as 1)
6.	use a formal written method of columnar addition (as 2)
7.	use a formal written method of columnar subtraction (as 2)
8.	use a formal written method of columnar addition with 3 numbers (as 2)
9.	use estimation to find the answer to a calculation (as 3)
10.	use inverse operation to check the answer to a calculation (as 3)
11.	solve a missing number problem (as 4)
12.	Explain how to solve a problem involving related number facts (as 4)
13.	solve a missing number problem involving place value (as 4)
14.	solve a two-step problem involving addition and subtraction (as 4)
15.	solve a problem involving more complex addition and subtraction (as 4)

Children's Scores

Percentages

Enlarge to A3 for added clarity

Please mark as

TEST
A B or C

Year 3: NUMBER - Multiplication and division

Children's Names

	Total correct per question	Percentage per question

Question Objectives

1. recall and use multiplication and division facts for the 3 times table (md 1)

2. recall and use multiplication and division facts for the 4 times table (md 1)

3. recall and use multiplication and division facts for the 8 times table (md 1)

4. connect the 2, 4 and 8 times tables through doubling (md 1)

5. use a mental method to multiply and divide a two-digit number by a one-digit number (md 1)

6. calculate a multiplication statement mentally including using commutativity (md 2)

7. calculate a multiplication statement mentally using associativity (md 2)

8. use multiplication or division facts to derive related facts (md 2)

9. use a formal written method to multiply a two-digit number by a one-digit number (md 2)

10. use a formal written method to divide a two or three-digit number by a one-digit number (md 2)

11. solve a problem involving multiplication (md 3)

12. solve a problem involving division (md 3)

13. solve a problem involving multiplication and scaling (md 3)

14. solve a problem involving multiplication and correspondence (md 3)

15. solve a problem involving division and correspondence (md 3)

Children's Scores

Percentages

Enlarge to A3 for added clarity

Year 3: NUMBER - Fractions

Please mark as

TEST

A B or C

Children's Names

	Total correct per question	Percentage per question

Question Objectives

1.	count up and down in tenths (f 1)		
2.	recognise that tenths arise from dividing an object into 10 equal parts (f 1)		
3.	match tenths to equivalent decimals (f 1)		
4.	divide a one-digit number by 10 (f 1)		
5.	find a fraction of a discrete set of objects (f 2)		
6.	identify the position of a mixed number on a number line (f 3)		
7.	recognise a fraction as part of a whole (f 3)		
8.	calculate and compare unit fractions of numbers (f 3)		
9.	find a unit fraction of a number (f 3)		
10.	recognise equivalent fractions with small denominators (f 4)		
11.	show equivalent fractions in shapes (f 4)		
12.	add fractions with the same denominator (f 5)		
13.	subtract fractions with the same denominator (f 5)		
14.	compare and order unit and non-unit fractions (f 6)		
15.	solve a problem involving addition of fractions (f 7)		

Children's Scores

Percentages

Enlarge to A3 for added clarity

Please mark as

TEST
A B or C

Year 3: MEASUREMENT

		Total correct per question	Percentage per question

Children's Names

Question Objectives

1. read a measure of length – cm/mm (m 1)

2. read a measure of mass – kg (m 1)

3. compare mixed unit measures – m/cm (m 1)

4. read a measure of capacity – ml (m 1)

5. add 3 quantities of mass – g (m 1)

6. add mixed units of capacity – l/ml (m 1)

7. measure the perimeter of a rectangle (m 2)

8. add and subtract amounts of money to give change (m 3)

9. add coins to find a total amount of money (m 3)

10. tell and write the time from an analogue clock including using Roman numerals from I to XII (m 4)

11. write the time on an analogue clock including translating from the 24-hour clock (m 4)

12. estimate and calculate time between 2 analogue clock times (m 5)

13. use vocabulary such as am/pm, morning/ afternoon, noon and midnight (m 5)

14. know the number of seconds in a minute and the number of days in each month, year and leap year (m 6)

15. calculate the time taken by an event (m 7)

Children's Scores

Percentages

Enlarge to A3 for added clarity

5

Year 3: GEOMETRY - Properties of shapes

Please mark as

TEST
A B or **C**

	Total correct per question	Percentage per question
Children's Names		

Question Objectives

1.	draw a rectangle (g 1)
2.	connect decimals and rounding to drawing and measuring straight lines in centimetres (g 1)
3.	match 3D shapes to their names (g 1)
4.	match 2D and 3D shapes to their descriptions (g 1)
5.	recognise angles as a property of shape (g 2)
6.	recognise angles as a description of a turn (g 2)
7.	describe turn as an amount of right angles (g 2)
8.	identify right angles (g 3)
9.	understand the relationship between right angles and amounts of turn (g 3)
10.	identify whether angles are greater than or less than a right angle (g 3)
11.	know the name of an angle that is greater than or less than a right angle (g 3)
12.	identify horizontal and vertical lines (g 4)
13.	draw a line perpendicular to an existing line (g 4)
14.	draw a line parallel to an existing line (g 4)
15.	identify lines that are perpendicular, parallel, horizontal or vertical (g 4)

Children's Scores

Percentages

Enlarge to A3 for added clarity

Please mark as

TEST
A B or C

Year 3: STATISTICS

Children's Names

	Total correct per question	Percentage per question

Question Objectives

1.	solve a one-step problem using information presented in a bar chart (s 2)
2.	solve a two-step problem using information presented in a bar chart (s 2)
3.	solve a multi-step problem using information presented in a bar chart (s 2)
4.	solve a one-step problem using information presented in a tally chart (s 2)
5.	solve a two-step problem using information presented in a tally chart (s 2)
6.	solve a multi-step problem using information presented in a tally chart (s 2)
7.	solve a two-step problem using information presented in a pictogram (s 2)
8.	solve a two-step problem using information presented in a pictogram (s 2)
9.	interpret and present data using a pictogram (s 1)
10.	solve a one-step problem using information presented in a frequency table (s 2)
11.	solve a two-step problem using information presented in a frequency table (s 2)
12.	interpret data using a frequency table (s 1)
13.	present data and solve a multi-step problem using information presented in a bar chart (s 2)
14.	interpret data using a bar chart (s 1)
15.	interpret data to determine the best way to present information (s 1)

Children's Scores

Percentages

Enlarge to A3 for added clarity

Name.. Class .... Date........................

NUMBER - Number and place value

Enter marks for each question (0, 1, 2) into the appropriate boxes to calculate percentage correct for each objective

npv1: count from 0 in multiples of 4, 8, 50 and 100; find 10 or 100 more or less than a given number
Q1 Q2 Q3 Q4 | %

npv2: recognise the place value of each digit in a three-digit number (hundreds, tens, ones)
Q5 | %

npv3: compare and order numbers up to 1000
Q6 | %

npv4: identify, represent and estimate numbers using different representations
Q7 | %

npv5: read and write numbers up to 1000 in numerals and in words
Q8 Q9 | %

npv6: solve number problems and practical problems involving these ideas
Q10 Q11 Q12 Q13 Q14 Q15 | %

TOTAL % SCORE %

NUMBER - Addition and subtraction

as1: add and subtract numbers mentally, including:
a) a three-digit number and ones
b) a three-digit number and tens
c) a three-digit number and hundreds
Q1 Q2 Q3 Q4 Q5 | %

as2: add and subtract numbers with up to three digits, using formal written methods of columnar addition and subtraction
Q6 Q7 Q8 | %

as3: estimate the answer to a calculation and use inverse operations to check answers
Q9 Q10 | %

as4: solve problems, including missing number problems, using number facts, place value, and more complex addition and subtraction
Q11 Q12 Q13 Q14 Q15 | %

TOTAL % SCORE %

NUMBER - Multiplication and division

md1: recall and use multiplication and division facts for the 3, 4 and 8 multiplication tables
Q1 Q2 Q3 Q4 Q5 | %

md2: write and calculate mathematical statements for multiplication and division using the multiplication tables that they know, including for two-digit numbers times one-digit numbers, using mental and progressing to formal written methods
Q6 Q7 Q8 Q9 Q10 | %

md3: solve problems, including missing number problems, involving multiplication and division, including positive integer scaling problems and correspondence problems in which *n* objects are connected to *m* objects
Q11 Q12 Q13 Q14 Q15 | %

TOTAL % SCORE %

continued on next page

continued from previous page

NUMBER - Fractions

f1:	count up and down in tenths; recognise that tenths arise from dividing an object into 10 equal parts and in dividing one-digit numbers or quantities by 10	Q1 Q2 Q3 Q4	**%**
f2:	recognise, find and write fractions of a discrete set of objects: unit fractions and non-unit fractions with small denominators	Q5	**%**
f3:	recognise and use fractions as numbers: unit fractions and non-unit fractions with small denominators	Q6 Q7 Q8 Q9	**%**
f4:	recognise and show, using diagrams, equivalent fractions with small denominators	Q10 Q11	**%**
f5:	add and subtract fractions with the same denominator within one whole (for example, $5/7 + 1/7 = 6/7$)	Q12 Q13	**%**
f6:	compare and order unit fractions, and fractions with the same denominators	Q14	**%**
f7:	solve problems that involve all of the above	Q15	**%**

TOTAL % SCORE   **%**

MEASUREMENT

m1:	measure, compare, add and subtract: lengths (m/cm/mm); mass (kg/g); volume/capacity (l/ml)	Q1 Q2 Q3 Q4 Q5 Q6	**%**
m2:	measure the perimeter of simple 2D shapes	Q7	**%**
m3:	add and subtract amounts of money to give change, using both £ and p in practical contexts	Q8 Q9	**%**
m4:	tell and write the time from an analogue clock, including using Roman numerals from I to XII, and 12-hour and 24-hour clocks	Q10 Q11	**%**
m5:	estimate and read time with increasing accuracy to the nearest minute; record and compare time in terms of seconds, minutes and hours; use vocabulary such as o'clock, a.m./p.m., morning, afternoon, noon and midnight	Q12 Q13	**%**
m6:	know the number of seconds in a minute and the number of days in each month, year and leap year	Q14	**%**
m7:	compare durations of events [for example to calculate the time taken by particular events or tasks]	Q15	**%**

TOTAL % SCORE   **%**

GEOMETRY - Properties of shapes / Position and direction

g1:	draw 2D shapes and make 3D shapes using modelling materials; recognise 3D shapes in different orientations and describe them	Q1 Q2 Q3 Q4	**%**
g2:	recognise angles as a property of shape or a description of a turn	Q5 Q6 Q7	**%**

continued on next page

continued from previous page

GEOMETRY - Properties of shapes / Position and direction *(continued)*

g3:	identify right angles, recognise that two right angles make a half-turn, three make three quarters of a turn and four a complete turn; identify whether angles are greater than or less than a right angle	☐ ☐ ☐ ☐ Q8 Q9 Q10 Q11	%
g4:	identify horizontal and vertical lines and pairs of perpendicular and parallel lines	☐ ☐ ☐ ☐ Q12 Q13 Q14 Q15	%

TOTAL % SCORE   %

STATISTICS

s1:	interpret and present data using bar charts, pictograms and tables	☐ ☐ ☐ ☐ Q9 Q12 Q14 Q15	%
s2:	solve one-step and two-step questions (for example, 'How many more?' and 'How many fewer?') using information presented in scaled bar charts and pictograms and tables	☐ ☐ ☐ ☐ ☐ ☐ Q1 Q2 Q3 Q4 Q5 Q6 ☐ ☐ ☐ ☐ ☐ Q7 Q8 Q10 Q11 Q13	%

TOTAL % SCORE   %

Test analysis software is also available from **HeadStart Primary**. Tests can be marked directly into the software; detailed performance analysis is then automatically generated for individuals, groups and classes.

Please visit **www.headstartprimary.com** for more information.